LIVE WELL:
Reveal Your Soul

Wanjohi Kibicho, Ph.D.

SAKATA
Publishers

Trenton, Canada

LIVE WELL: Reveal Your Soul

Copyright © 2022 Wanjohi Kibicho, Ph.D.

Apart from any fair dealing for the purpose of research or private study, or criticism or review, as permitted under the Copyright, Designs and Patents Act 1988, this publication may only be reproduced, stored or transmitted, in any form or by any means, with prior permission in writing of the copyright owner. Enquiries concerning reproduction outside these terms should be sent to the publisher at the undermentioned address:

71 Murphy St,
Trenton, Ontario,
K8V 0C3
CANADA

Published by Sakata Publishers
Trenton, Canada 2022

ISBN- 978-1-9991291-2-5
ISBN- 978-1-9991291-3-2

Printed and bound by Lulu, USA

Dedication

To: Sephora Kibicho - My Mother

You infused life into me: Life from the heavens.
You taught me to dream: Dream to accomplish.
You showed me the way: The way of the wise.
You taught me right from wrong.
Towards the right, you unfailingly pushed me.

O' mama, you're my Angel.
The Angel that birthed me.
Guides, shelters and restores me.
Whene'er lost, your unfailin' love,
Uplifts 'n shows me the way.
With an open heart 'n endurin' fortitude,
You give me all.
My superhero you're:
A touchstone for my values!

Dearest mama, you're Angelic – gentle yet strong.
E'er patient whene'er I'm foolish.
A dependable source of comfort whene'er I fall short.
Today, your feet might feel like weights.
But, through the miles you have covered,
You've shown me the way.
You've sown the seed of love.
For like moonshine,
Your love transforms the savage into beauty.
My heart overflows with love for you.

[My mother passed on three days before the publication of this book]

To: Maria Kibicho - My Light

A woman of reverence, she is.
Defined by the flash of her eyes; and,
Curl of her chest.
Exemplified by the span of her hips;
Swing of her waist 'n stride of her steps.
Formin' an angelic form.

Her inner wonderment's unreachable.
Topped off with an intelligent mind 'n a glamorous heart.
Illuminated by the fire in her soul; and,
The sun of her smile.
Characterized by the elegance of her stye; and,
The grace of her existence.
A woman who knows when to advance or retreat;
Knows how to sing 'n dance.
In saintly way.

She's ultimate:
A poise 'n deportment that no sculptor can capture.
She's the real deal:
The root of the root;
The bud of the bud; and,
The sky of the sky.
A wonder that glues stars together.
Generatin' a serene scene.
A scene that births sanity.
For, she' calm 'n well-possessed of herself.
A nobly planned gentlewoman,
Who breathes thoughtful breaths.
A lady with a firm reason 'n temperate will;
Skill 'n foresight of a virtuous being.
Maria, she is!
The Deity's crownin' master piece.

To: Karen, Wesley 'n Serena Kibicho - My Stars

Rooted in a perpetual place - my heart.
They're the loveliest kids e'er born:
Beauty at its finest.
Hearts of angels;
Souls so pure 'n sweet.
Whatever they do is full of flowers:
Smile to the waters – waves of love rise;
Touch the Earth - seeds of grace swell.
They're magical…
They're my North Star.
They're: Sephora, Naftie 'n Fancey.

> My dear Stars,
> You reside at the apex of my being - heart 'n soul.
> You shower me with jollity each day.
> You're my best friends 'n teachers of life.
> For, you taught me how to fall decently when skatin';
> And, how not to be hanged when playin' Hangman.
> My life has ne'er been so complete.
> I declare thence:
> Love you three - more than me.

>> My Stars keep doing well what you do.
>> Fear only fear itself.
>> Boldly venture into the unventured caves 'n castles.
>> For, all are strangers before they're friends.
>> So, feet on the ground 'n eyes skyward,
>> Speak your mind…
>> …And create the world you dream of.

To: My Family - broadly defined

Sailed upon the seven seas 'n slept in e'ery land:
Lazed 'n searched (in) the Antarctic...
Loved 'n gamed in Australia...
Swam 'n grew in Japan...
Learnt, laughed 'n made babies in France...
Taught 'n dreamt in South Africa...
Lolled 'n forgot in the Caribbean shores...
Thrived, loved 'n made (more) babies in Canada...
Lounged 'n explored (in) the Arctic...
O' yeah! Wonders of the world I've witnessed.
But, I've seen no other you.

O' dear - special you're - to me.
You're a sweet melody - always sooth my mind.
You're a fireside-circle - unbreakable.
Oceans-mountains-valleys apart;
But, a part of you leaves me not.
As you flow in my veins.
Makin' me live life of profundity 'n become a better me.

Sharin' the past, present 'n future,
We're a family with infinite memories.
Memories of love 'n tears - laughter 'n fears...
When down - let's pick each other.
When lost - let's guide each other.
When forlorn - let's uplift each other.
Through merriment 'n sorrow:
Lets shower each other with good-will.
Through joy 'n anguish:
Let's bask in unshakable bond of kinship.
In our bodies, hearts 'n souls,
May our adoration for each other run deep.

To: My Progenitors

As I sit silently watchin' the moon above,
I wonder at her beauty 'n my past kin.
I wonder how my past kin,
Sat 'n admired the (same) moon in her softly healin' light.
I wonder how my future kin,
Will repeat this rite on a softly moonlit night.
And as I contemplate on her beauteous light;
And glorious silver path.
I bring together past 'n future on this present night.
For, from 'em emerged a trunk 'n branches.
Branches from which our ways commenced.
So, when we see their images - we see selves.
As we carry 'em in us.
Cause their songs are our songs;
And, our songs are our children's songs.

O' progenitors,
You stare across the space at me.
I know your eyes - you know mine.
I know your soul - you know mine.
I'm all of you - you're all of me;
Bestowin' e'ery grain of sand brushin' against my palms a story.
A story 'n a block to build upon for morrow's generation.
For, when we illuminate the road back to our forebears,
They manifest selves prettily.
For, a family tree can wither not if tended.
And, as Marcus Cicero (106 - 43 BC) teaches me:
We're immortal till our stories die.
For, anyone who gives love,
Lives on in another's heart.

 No self stands alone.
Behind it stretches an endless chain,
To which it belongs 'n which it carries on.
No self's of itself alone.

It has an extended link of ancestors.
- This is an eternal memory not a mere allegory -
For, when we connect with our past,
We evolve collective consciousness;
And, we infuse ancient truths into the future.
As we proffer guideposts to those who follow.
For, no self stands alone 'n one can live without the other not:
Each is the other's hope, meanin' 'n strength.
And, a generation carries the pain,
So that the next can live 'n heal.

Acknowledgement

To all children from underprivileged backgrounds. You are my heroes. For, collectively, you teach me:
> Violent winds do not blow all day;
> And, snowstorm cannot fall all day
> So, if you're on the way – be the way.

A special acknowledgement goes to my model, President Nelson Mandela (1918 – 2013). A model who taught me:
> Strength lies in our differences.
> So, as we embark on Live Well journey,
> Let's embrace each other's uniqueness.
> And, let truth speak through you - with respect.

A special word of gratitude is due to Nicole Perras. Your acts when my world was 'leaking' proved to me that:
> Luck's not a factor.
> Hope's not a strategy;
> And, fear's not an option.

A note of acknowledgement goes to Judy Hersey. Through many hours conversing on the structure of this book, I came to conclude that:
> Hard depends on soft 'n little on more.
> High's tested by low 'n crooked by straight.
> Long's determined by low 'n worn by new.
> Back's defined by front 'n day by night.

To Monika Geant, your words of wisdom never fail. I'll forever remember the following lines:
> In movement seek stillness.
> In stillness seek rest.
> In rest be mindful.

Throughout, be attentive at that infinite moment where the future becomes the past.

To everyone at Sakata Publishers for providing the space for the seeds of my thoughts to unknowingly germinate. Your careful editing and questions on tone and approach made this book better. Thus, I wholly embrace your teachings:
>Be like heaven.
>Drip sweet dew.
>Equally to all, with no regulation.

To Maria Kibicho, with more than I could ever imagine. For showing up at River Kingston and showing up every hour since. Everything good in me exists because of you. Your presence teaches me:
>Knowing others' intelligent.
>Knowing self's enlightenment.
>Conquering self's true strength.

To my martial arts Sensei, Morihei Ueshiba (1883 - 1969), for sparkling a fire in my brain. A fire that I didn't know it existed; and that no one will ever put off. I still hear your life-changing lesson: We gain by losing and lose by gaining.

Dear reader, as we together embark on this journey code named, *Live Well*, I bow to you and say:
>No enemy can harm you;
>As much as your own thoughts, unguarded.
>Empathize with the unawakened;
>And, your innate light will shine-out, effortlessly.
>Subdue yourself, and you will discover your inner divinity.
>Tread gently, purposefully and lovingly;
>Leave only graceful heart-prints and no half-formed impressions.

Wanjohi Kibicho, Ph.D.
Ottawa, Canada,
December 2022

Foreword: Poetry is Life in Words

Poetry is painting that is felt rather than seen;
And, painting is poetry that is seen rather than felt.
  ~ Leonardo Da Vinci (1452 – 1519) ~

Poetry is finer and more philosophical than history;
For poetry expresses the universal,
And history only the particular.
  ~ Aristotle (384 – 322) ~

To let off steam 'n concentrate mind to the wonders of life,
Nelson Mandela (1918 – 2013) practiced boxing;
Leonardo da Vinci (1452 – 1519) played music;
Abraham Lincoln (1809 – 1865) told stories;
While Charles Darwin (1809 – 1882) dined on exotic animals.

To unwind 'n connect with nature,
Louis Pasteur (1822 – 1895) painted;
Thomas Edison (1847 – 1931) made fireworks;
Oscar Wilde (1854 – 1900) 'n George Orwell (1903 – 1950) learnt foreign tongues;
While Vincent Van Gogh (1853 – 1890) consumed alcohol.

To relax 'n attain inner peace,
Nikolay Gumilyov (1886 – 1921) collected African artefacts;
Ingrid Bergman (1915 - 1982) documented her letters;
John Lennon (1940 – 1980) played Monopoly;
While Sigmund Freud (1856 – 1939) 'n Fidel Castro (1926 – 2016) smoked fat cigars.

To decompress 'n inject life into my life,
I compose poems.
For, poetry's life in words.

A word of confession though: I do not write poetry for publication. I write for the same reason that, according to Ingrid Bergman, one should document a diary, to have something private to read when happy and when sad. So, I write to:

Connect the body with the mind;
Connect the mind with the soul;
Connect the body with the soul.
I write to speak to inner me;
And, to relax.

Poetry has a natural place in all stages of our lives. Thus, we know far more poetry than we think we do. For, poetry is a primal impulse within all human beings. At tender age thus, we were thrilled and startled by the effects of poetry. As kindergarteners, we tasted words through chants; heard rhymes through music; and felt rhythms as we danced. Encountering poetry at an older age have an equally visceral and compelling effect. This modest compilation of poems will be a testimony to the foregoing. It is set out to fulfil that daily need. It will accompany you through the ups and downs of life.

A good poem calms tormented souls, smoothens rough relationships, soothes the bereaved, seduces the hesitant and lulls unfatigued baby to sleep. For, poems allow us to say what we really mean especially when dealing with out of the ordinary happenings. Poetry is not afraid of colouring raw facts of life: sex, birth, life and death. It enables the writer to explain the unexplainable as poetry is as accurate as nature. It is more passionate than a lover; more honest than a confidant; and, braver than an adversary. It has the power to mention what the world's too polite to mention.

Poems are carriers of dreams, knowledge and wisdom. Well thought of words bring understanding making time and timelessness to live together. They shoot at the barriers of the unknown and the unknowable. Poetry unveils the hidden beauty of the world making the unfamiliar familiar and the limited limitless. For it has the power to deal with any subject and tell any story.

As we embark on this journey together, I urge you, and I am on my knees here, not to hold poems that calm you down, let you escape daily life, or reassure you – in lower esteem than poems that unsettle you, or challenge you. They are all equally relevant as we sometimes need support when dealing with today's frightening vagaries of life.

The encounter may at times be uncomfortable but, like a genuine friend, a book of poems should offer shocks and support by shaking you out of your usual way of thinking. It should inspire you to extend your horizon of life by compelling you to:
- Look at yourself upside-down and inside-out. This will give colourful expression to your feelings.
- Hear words you would rather not hear. This will inject flavour to your journey of life.
- See things you would rather not see. This will push you up against the flames of life.

For, poetry says what cannot be forthrightly said. And, as Thomas Gray (1716 – 1771) tells us: "poems are thoughts that breathe and words that burn…"

The scene of this modest tale is laid amid humble localities that I lived. In these localities, I have seen and heard beauty in the simple. I have touched, smelt and felt the beautiful in the simple. Therefore, with utmost humility, I invite you to open your eyes and look with me – through reading the pages that follow. I ask you to look at: the children, the sky, the trees, the birds, the hills, the valleys, the rocks, the lakes, the rivers, the seas; and, see what is good and true in them. You will see their goodliness through a magnifying lens by joining me in this journey code named: *Live Well – Reveal Your Soul*.

Poetry is not read like story books in which the text carries a single message. Thus, the reader absorbs the message and moves on to the next section. In poetry, words are used differently – concentrated and often intense. Consequently, the reader needs to feel, hear, taste, touch and smell their rhythm, shape and balance. To understand the connections and combinations of the poems therefore, I urge you to take your time: savour every word; taste every line. For, like in the old art of chocolate eating, it is less enjoyable to bite big chunks and swallow them whole - untasted. Instead, nibble a small piece, allow it to slowly melt inside you as it infuses into you, blends with you and becomes you. Similarly, savour every word in this compilation and be the journey.

So, read the pieces in this book as slowly as you possibly can.
Savour the words.
Taste the rhythm.
See the shape.
Enjoy the balance.
And, I assure you; this is more rewarding than snapping-off huge chunks and swallow them whole. Thence, grab a pencil and make marks on the poems as you progress.

Throughout derive pleasure through luxurious engagement with the words, rhythms and acts. Feel the physical, the sensual, the textural, the voice, the weight, the density, the euphony and the tactile aspects of the written and uttered words. Investigate new shapes and new incidents that emerge in your body, mind and soul.

Ying-Yang: the Conceptual Framework

As used in this modest volume, the ying-yang relationship indicates that the universe is governed by a cosmic duality. These sets of two opposing and complementing principles can be observed in nature: day and night; dark and light; sun and moon; male and female; hard and soft; high and low; cold and hot; passive and active.

Ying and yang are not static or mutually exclusive. Rather, their nature lies in the interchange and interplay of the two components. For, the world is composed of many different opposing forces that can easily coexist and even complement each other. In fact, oftentimes, forces opposite in nature rely on one another to exist. A good example is the alternation of day and night: there cannot be a shadow without light.

The ying-yang balance is important and indeed omnipresent in nature. Their interplay on one another, as one increases the other decreases, being a description of the actual process of the universe and all that is in it. From a physical viewpoint, in emptiness forms exist. Without emptiness form cannot exist and emptiness cannot be validated without form. For example, without the hole (emptiness) a doughnut (form/fullness) cannot exist.; without a void space (emptiness) a pot (form) cannot exist. This is the philosophical base on which the Universe exists. It helps us transcend the time-space constraints. For, pain and pleasure are two bells, when one sounds, the other knells.

The Book: *Live Well – Reveal Your Soul*

Within the thirty-two chapters that follow, the poems are organized by what they say. Addressing specific themes of life allows the poems to speak to each other, which is an arduous task in poetry. For, a poem may be talking about jollity at the same time as sadness; or, birth at the same time as death; or, immortal at the same time mortal.

Consequently, the categories are fluid. Each chapter aims to derive home a selected message. The lifeline that this anthology maps out is thus personal but not in any way prescriptive. Subsequently, you can read continuously, or you can take each chapter like a lucky dip, chose it, read it and enjoy it. Or, you can rummage about until you find the poem that fits your frame of mind. Or, randomly pick a poem and let it fly you to unexpected destination.

Throughout this journey, you will encounter an astonishing rich amalgam of symbolic images from birth to death. The surreal sensibility of life lived well is recapitulated – synthesized and harmonized with the least forcing. The intentional intermixture of the sensibility of ups and downs, twists and turns of life is evident in both the attitudes and the tone of the poems, which is heavily musical and rhythmic.

When reading a poem, I love to understand a little background:
- What is the scene described in the poem?
- What provoked the poet to write this piece?
- Did the writer live his later days in contentment?

Consequently, I have given some incidental details on some selected poems, which – I hope -, illuminate the lovely words you are about to savour.

I start this journey with a heartily note to you dear reader: I derived enormous pleasure from writing the one hundred and sixty nine poems in this collection; and, like anyone with passion, I am delighted to share it with you. And, I hope that you will have as much fun dipping into the book as I had compiling it.

Like in the case of all my published work, 100% of the proceeds from the sale of this book go to charity in support of the underprivileged children. In which case, I thank you for buying a copy of this book, as it will have a direct positive effect on a poor and deprived child's wellbeing on this earth.

Table of Contents

DEDICATION	I
ACKNOWLEDGEMENT	VII
FOREWORD: POETRY IS LIFE IN WORDS	IX
TABLE OF CONTENTS	XV
PART ONE	**1**
LIFE	3
CHILDHOOD	15
HUMANITY	23
INTEGRITY	31
RESILIENCE	37
LOVE	49
HOPE	63
FAIRNESS	71
HUMILITY	77
NOBILITY	83
REST	87
DEDICATION	91
DIVERSITY	95
APPRECIATION	101
FORGIVENESS	107
FRIENDSHIP	111
HAPPINESS	123
GOODLINESS	129
FEMININITY	135
PARENTHOOD	141
BEAUTY	147
CHARACTER	151
WELL WISHES	157
PART TWO	**167**
EGOTISM	169
POOR LEADERSHIP	173
GREEDINESS	183

HYPOCRISY 189
MEDIOCRITY 195
PREJUDICE 199
HATRED 215
PANDEMIC 221
DEATH 231
PART THREE 253
END 255
REFERENCES 259
ABOUT THE AUTHOR 261

PART ONE

YING OF LIFE

Chapter 1

Life

*Life is a series of natural and spontaneous changes.
Don't resist them – that only creates sorrow.
Let reality be reality.
Let things flow naturally forward in whatever way they like.*

~ Lao Tzu (571 – 447 BC) ~

1.1 Let the Daughter and Son of Zeus Converse

A soul free of impediment – 'tis you!
You inject colors of vibrancy onto life:
Pink 'n Blue the better.
You infuse colors of vivacity onto beingness:
Pink 'n Pink – difference's the same.
You infuse colors of jollity:
Blue 'n Blue – no difference.
You're miracle…
Pink 'n Blue, that's the miracle.
Feel, hear, see, smell 'n taste it in your song.

Ready to sing lullabies night long.
As life lives on,
Inside nature's souvenir crystal balls.
Souvenirs inside you,
Awaitin' to see, express 'n hold.
Eyes yet to open with delight...
Mouths full of expressions untold...
Hands ready to hold...
A little kick 'n a soft wriggle inside.
A beautiful bump 'n a bit of mornin' nausea.
That's the miracle – in the makin'.

Worry not dear one:
For, that's the inner glow that you harbour.
That's the daughter 'n son of Zeus conversin' (with you).
Just know:
The wait will be memorable;
And, the result will be reverential.
So, savor every second of this miracle in the makin'.

1.2 Life is a Journey

Compare self not with others.
For, competin' with others, makes us bitter;
While, competin' with ourselves, makes us better.
Our differences make each of us special.
Allow not your life slip by livin' in the past.
For, livin' in the past kills present;
While, livin' in the moment fosters future.
And, life is a journey to be savoured stepwise.

Embrace your imperfections.
For, 'tis the thread of fragility that binds us together.
And, I can ne'er be what I ought to be;
'Til you're what you ought to be.

Dismiss not your dreams.
For, being dreamless is to be hopeless.
And, to be hopeless is to be purposeless.
So, let's share dreams 'n shape our purpose.
For, we're united in network of mutuality.
In the journey of life;
Towards a common destiny.

1.3 Revert to the Fundamentals

Confucius (551 - 479 BC) teaches:
The mooncalf lives in the extraordinary.
He imagines of a vivid flash of lightnin';
Roll of thunder 'n crashin' of hail;
Happenin' in concert…
He makes life complex.
Conversely, the wiser moves in the direction of ordinary.
He finds the universal elements sufficient.
Finds air 'n water exhilaratin'.
He's thrilled by rain 'n night-stars;
And, refreshed by morning strolls 'n evening saunters.
He's elated o'er a bird's nest 'n a wildflower in spring.
He's aroused by the basics.

> Since the genesis - the blueprint's clear:
> The questioning's the same - only answers differ…
> No demands are too great to bear -
> The basics will suffice…
> So, why adjective up your life?
> Be - Just be.
> And, the laws of the Universe will be plain.
> Just be, 'n you'll see no need to paint the sky blue.
> Just be, 'n you'll see no need to coax the Sun to rise.
> Just be, 'n you'll see no need to order flowers to bloom.
> Just be, 'n you'll see no need to teach birds to sing.
> Just be, 'n you'll see no need to counsel lovers how to kiss.
> Just be…

>> Lose not the day in expectation of the night,
>> And, night in fear of the dawn.
>> Just be…

And, live in harmony with the Universe
By embracin' the basics.
The wisdom of life lies in the elimination of non-essentials.
Supress thus, the unnecessary so that the necessary speaks.
Starve non-essentials 'n walk the miracle mile,
'Til you see your name lighted in the northern lights.
Listen to the Universe 'n learn from the stars.
Relax 'n float down the river of life,
And, shed your cocoon into a beautiful butterfly.
As sparkles of the Universe are you…
…Just revert to the fundamentals.

1.4 Success is in the Dreams we Weave

Life's alive with heroism:
Un-trumpeted 'n trumpeted;
Unreal 'n real.
Real heroism's laborin' good on good to fix.
'Tis slitherin' placidly amid the haste 'n noise;
And, listenin' to all.
For, e'en the dull have a story…
None-the-less, avoidin' the loud 'n the aggressive –
As they are vexations to tranquil soul.

Real success' in the dreams we weave 'n the stories we tell.
The hearts we touch 'n the minds we awaken.
'Tis hallmarked by the sincerity in our laughter;
And, the solemnity in our griefs.
Reflected in the purity of our souls 'n ne'er the size of our zircons.
Success basks in the respect of the sages;
And, the admiration of the children.
For, he who looks for the good in others,
He who appreciates nature's unrefined beauty…
His life's an inspiration.
And, through him truth speaks.

All can be skippers not – crew, some must be.
But, the task at hand remains near 'n dear.
So, if you can't be a muscallonge then be a bass –
The liveliest 'n loveliest bass in the

bayou!
Compare not your perfections to
imperfections of the other.
Rather, open your scroll 'n centre on
your destiny.
Throughout, dance with wildness…

1.5 Better to Journey Well than to Arrive

Some stories lack a clear head or tail-end.
As life's a delicious ambiguity.
It can only be understood backwards;
But must be lived forwards.
Life's a beautiful thingy.
Some *faux pas* 'n absurdities no doubt;
A fresh beginning's promised though…
Begin it serenely.

Life's in your triumphs 'n failures;
In your tears 'n fears.
Life's what you make (of) it – live it!
Life's your teacher – love it!
Life's a fantastic dream - be it!
Be a deep lake: Calm still surface but great depths of kindness.
As, to a still soul, Universe surrenders.
But, if you know not to which port you're sailin',
No wind's favourable.

Adopt the secret of Nature: *Patience*.
Emulate her stratagem: *Nothing's perfect 'n everything's perfect*.
Imperfection defines her exhilaratin' beauty.
So, sing not 'cause you've to sing.
Sing 'cause you've a song to sing.
Like a song thrush thence, sing towards creative pursuits -
Unconcerned about who hears.
And, nurture your innate paladin.
As, the life you fantasize's real.
Just love self in all your frailties.
For, 'tis better to journey well than to arrive.

1.6 On *Agura* Atop of Life

Twenty years 'n already enamoured…
I listened o'er 'n again to the cantata.
The one that held the key to my very beingness…
Through its music's dance,
Not just a mere farewell to a natural world.
A world of uncultured flowers 'n flocks of birds,
On the saintly plains of Chepkoilel pampas.
Plains where I discovered the ecstasy of word-rhymes.
Rhythm wedded to melodic contour;
Held in place by voice 'n touch of harmony.
On *agura* atop youth[fullness]…

> O' youth!
> The wiser who's yet to proof his foolishness.
> Know it all - untaught:
> How ground-mole sinks his well;
> And, how oriole hangs her nest.
> Where the wood-grape's clusters shine;
> And, where to insert the finger – in darkness.
> Painless play with health that mocked the physician's rules.
> *Oh ja*: we were rich in hummingbirds 'n wild-flowers.
> For our game - honeybees gamed.

>> Announced by the trumpets of the sky.
>> Un(fore)warned by Nature's geometric signs.
>> The gray day zig-zagged;
>> Crossed, cris-crossed 'n re-criss-crossed,
>> Expandin' my horizon.
>> No walls of firmament:
>> No cloud above - no earth below.

As the horizon swelled,
My mental-festal dainties fulminated,
Like a regal tent upon shriekin' mindless wind kissin' heat.
Today, a gray man:
Smooched by multiracial-berries;
And radiant with a mimic flame.
Through 'n with a jaunty grace thence I bestow –
Outward sunshine - inward joy.
For, I was once a faceless-titleless boy!
On *agura* atop youth-full-ness…

> Truth for truth 'n good for good!
> For truth's good for good.
> Twisted hard in mortal agony of born unborn.
> So, I taunt Diogenes' thoughts,
> And weep in Zeno's fangs.
> For, I remember how we made the coldness visible.
> As we let the coastal-wind roar back with tropical heat…
> O' time 'n change!
> With grayness -
> Who cares how the night behaved?
> Who cares how the firelight raved?
> Why die thence-fore with a heart-bleedin' ill-will?
> Blow high - blow low!
> No voice's heard - no sign's made.
> Yet, faith trusts 'n love dreams.
> And, the wild wide earth's o'er,
> …But, we're one!
> On *agura* atop life.

1.7 Unmatched

You're unmatched.
You're ahead of the game;
And, you'll soar skyward.

For you're so filled with life.
Life free of prejudice 'n ill-will.
Your infectious positivity is hard not to feel.

And, in the midst of gloom,
Your authentic smiles make days more humane.
But, I'm happy that your dreams are seein' the Sun.

1.8 Lovely Life

Enjoy the infinite pleasure of a sticky cheek-kiss;
Be amazed at the beauty of emptiness;
And, make the ordinary come alive.
For, with all its drudgery;
And, unattained dreams;
'Tis still a lovely life.
Lovely life.
Life.

Chapter 2

Childhood

*Do not train a child to learn by harshness.
Instead, direct them to it by what amuses their minds.
That way, you will discover with accuracy,
The peculiar bent of the genius of each.*

~ Plato (424 - 348 BC) ~

2.1 I Am Child

My readers ask me: who are you?

I'm like a child.
A child who:
Loves wild flowers;
Loves smell of freshly mowed grass;
And, loves the caress of the wintery wind.

A simple mortal,
Who loves the spontaneity of a child.
A mortal who:
Trusts to be trusted;
Respects to be respected;
And, loves to be loved.

A mere earthling;
Made entirely of flaws.
Flaws stitched together;
But, with good intentions.
For, I'm like a child without being a child.
A fallibilist who believes in fallibilism.

2.2 Child's a Child: Pure and Virginal

Whirlwinds, we're born with.
Able to sing to birds;
And, see destiny in snowflakes.
For, seen with a young's eye,
Nature's lucid 'n resplendent.
As children are superior to any balladry e'er composed.
Livin' poetry in the realm of love - they're.

In children's magical realm;
There's joy 'n trust,
Eternal bliss 'n cheer.
For, a child's purpose is to be a child.
As, a song once sung,
Is no longer a song;
And, dance once danced,
Is no longer a dance.
A child's a child: pure 'n virginal.

Check not a youngling with terror.
Lest you dam a flowin' river.
Guide it through the valleys.
Trace its rivulet's in the sand,
And, let its swellings revive the withered land.
Trim 'n train its tendershoots;
Bend 'n fold its tendertwigs;
And, mould it to essentials of life.
Allow it act silly;
And, come into communion with the hard Sun of logic.
Let it taste heartsad as its juvenile reason wilts;
And, usher it into the divinity of being.
As children are future…

2.3 Children are Sons and Daughters of Life

Parenthood's a glorious *métier*.
For, parents are life-bows.
Bows from which children as livin' arrows are set-forth.
The Archer, He who oversees the path of/to the infinite,
Bends them that the arrows travel smooth-swift 'n far.
And, as He loves arrows that fly steady;
He also relishes bows that are stable.
Thence, let your bendin' in His able hands be for gladness.
As, you're only the designated life-bow.
And, children are sons 'n daughters of life:
They come through you - not from you;
You house their bodies - not their souls.
For, their souls dwell in the house of future;
And, life's experienced backward but lived forward.

> For children's fragile souls, offer them a heart of patience.
> For their innocent mistakes, accord them a head of coolness.
> So, speak with reason 'n act with stainless heart;
> And, they'll listen 'n love you.
> Tell them 'n they'll forget;
> Teach them 'n they may remember;
> But, involve them 'n they learn.
> For, they aren't good at listenin' to their idols;
> But ne'er fail to imitate them.
> As such, be a model worth imitation.
> For, you don't teach virtue by preachin' virtue.
> Rather, you teach virtue by actin' virtuous.

>> Discipline but ne'er punish the younglings...
>> For, parental discipline's about love;

While punishment's an outburst of negative energy.
An act that can't reverse the aftermath of the season of violence.
Make 'em not slaves of praise;
Say a 'no' to 'em as an act of love…
And, you give 'em quintessential tools,
To face the turns 'n twists of life.
Be in their lives today;
And, you'll be in their memories tomorrow.
Keep them closer when they're young,
And, they'll keep you closer when [you'll be] old.

2.4 Your Children's Mistakes are Your Mistakes

A child's mind's a *tabula rasa*.
A pure potentiality that's actualized through livin'.
Impress on it worthy things...
Lest, it be impressed pleasurably with images of lesser worth.
For, parenting's like tunin' a guitar cord.
If too loose, it generates unrefined music;
But, snaps under great tension.
Tuned well, with encouragement 'n tolerance;
Children learn confidence 'n patience.
While with acceptance 'n honesty;
They learn endearment 'n truthfulness.
And, in security, they nurture faith in self 'n others.
They know when to give-in gracefully;
And, when to act tough.

Conversely, under asketh 'n thou receive rule;
Where freedom equates no rules...
Multi-headed soulless hydras are born;
Hallmarked by super-bloated heads 'n hyper-inflated egos.
Confined in their skunky skull-sized hell,
They burn with entitlement 'n bluster.
In the burnin', they see e'ery adversity as an injustice;
And, e'ery challenge as a failure.
They take e'ery inconvenience as a personal slight;
And, e'ery disagreement as a betrayal...
So, like incandescent bugs,
With bulgin' eyes 'n antennaes more twisted than Twizzlers
They willingly make full-contact with Chryslers -
Cruisin' at hundred-seventeen kilometres an hour!
The only way they understand that superheroes are rare.

O' parents your children's mistakes are your mistakes,
But, the death toll will be heavier for them.
A toll that will dim the edges of e'ery jollity you've e'er seen.
Antidote:
Induct them to the art of holdin' passion.
Edify them:
Pain's a central thread in the fabric of life;
And, tearin' it off unravels more destructive pains.
Let them know:
Like a path untaken,
'Tis the pain absorbed that makes the difference.
Tell them:
The river of life comprises of lights 'n shadows,
And, 'tis asinine to wish of no shadows.

Notes on the Poems
Humanhood's imperfect!
Parenthood excellently magnifies the foregoin'.
But, as a parent you're only in competition with self:
To be a better parent today than yesterday;
And, a better parent tomorrow than today.
Un meilleur progéniteur à tout jamais!

2.5 Our Lives' Anchors

Our archer sees the path of the infinite;
He bends us so that his arrows go smooth and far.
But, as He loves the arrows that fly;
So does He, the bows that are solid.

Thence, let our bending in his hand be of contentment.
Our children are our lives' anchors.
Let's therefore give them roots 'n wings.
Let's not toughen them up to face a heartless world;
But, raise children who'll make the world less heartless.

Our children are more than the sum of their accomplishments.
Hence, let's love them for more than their abilities.
For, e'en when they seem to be the most vexatious tiny blisters;
They're wonderful.
They're lovely!

Chapter 3

Humanity

Humanity is the quality,
Which stops one being arrogant,
Towards one's fellows;
Or being acrimonious.
...All cruelty springs from weakness.

~ Seneca the Younger (4 BC – 65 AD) ~

3.1 People of Benignity

Let's be people of benignity;
People of hope;
And, beacons of light.
People who support,
Sing 'n laugh.

Let's be people of benignity.
Let's do it by:
Maintainin' physical distance;
But, preservin' social connection.
Let's do this by:
Findin' opportunities to support 'n to praise;
Findin' apologias to sing 'n to dance.
And, findin' latitudes,
To laugh 'n to love.

Let's be beacons of light;
People of hope -
People of benignity.
People who praise,
Dance 'n love.

3.2 Sewn Together with Unbreakable Thread

Comin' from the same place - goin' to the same place:
E'ery being's a blueprint.
Humanity - seekers of knowledge call it.
Hear her euphoric nature in the wind 'n sea.
As *my* humanity's bound-up in *yours*,
And, we can only be human together.
For, like islands in the ocean; we're unconnected on the surface,
but connected in the deep.
Sewn together with unbreakable thread.
A thread of humanity.

Unbowed by the winds of resistance thence,
Let's slow our pace 'n enable our thoughts to float heavenward;
And, allow humanity be what she ought to be.
Let's rise beyond the narrow confines of individualistic concerns.
And, dissolve the dark odds violatin' her.
Let's be rays of hope 'n guide her to self-realization.
In earnest 'n with purity of reverence, let's be the reason someone
believes in the goodness in humanity…
Let's together, make humanity shine on - again.

Awaken self to awaken humanity.
March with the Sun-Moon synchronicity;
Walk in resolve of light-casters - firm 'n solid;
And, let humanity gather greatness 'n grandeur.
Announce the comin' of a new dawn,
A dawn that reinstates *the Ying-Yang* of life;
That rebalances light 'n darkness…
And, let the Universe utter the magical words:
As within so without - as above so below;
Let it be so - humanity shines on…

3.3 Our Conjoined Genesis

Your combined beauty's truth.
In its presence,
Space shudders 'n time unfurls:
The far becomes near;
While, the past becomes now.
In your presence,
Matter coalesces transformin' the waves tween us...
Transformin' our shared waves into magical symphonic melody.
Melody meeker than a fine-tuned piccolo pearl.
Mild sounds that exact focus o'er us all.
As we become what we ought to be – unique.

> Originality's returnin' to the origin.
> For, with no appreciation of our source –
> Rootless trees we become.
> Bemused by Homeric external virtues –
> Mere witnesses of life we become.
> But nay, this *Island* thinks of you in the day;
> Thinks of you at night 'n time in-tween
> For, this *Island* reveres your cold breeze in the day;
> And, venerates your warmth at night.
> As, this *Island* cherishes our conjoined genesis;
> And, is prideful of your pristine hearts 'n radiant smiles.
> Smiles that tame the beneath currents,
> Towards an eternal bliss.

> > Heard melodies are sweet –
> > The unheard e'en sweeter.
> > So, let your soothin' pipes play on;
> > Not to the sensual ear;
> > But to the spirit ditties of no tone;

And, for e'er wilt not thou love.
Say what you mean 'n do what you say.
Shoot straight - no crab dancin'.
Stand for the logical truth - no dogmatic fantasies.
And, for e'er wilt not thou love.

3.4 To Serve not to be Served

Swayin' in the clouds at 1,700 nautical miles,
I blithely 'n proudly join this cheerful dissonance of psychedelia.
To sing your melodious song.
Be forewarned though: Much remains unsaid 'n undone;
Pages unturned 'n questions unasked.
As, your election win's mere risin' of the Sun.
A ticket for your journey to service: To serve not to be served.

With neither remorse nor randomness,
Restrain not your aroused huntin' instincts.
To appease the twisted nympholepsy.
Rather, employ them usefully.
Hunt alone – if need be;
And, let no pettifoggin' rules dampen your resolve.
Hide not your selfhood:
A proof that you're free from maraudin' dark forces.
Have the courage to pleasantly,
And, unapologetically say no.
No to advances that corrode your genuine Yes.
Honour that good promise you ne'er made.

Objects in motion stay in motion,
'Til they encounter a resistin' force.
Keep the momentum forward.
Spread your wings;
And, shine like shells of scarlet.
Gleam like the dusky splendours of evenin' clouds.
Glimmer like unwaverin' flame in the half-light of an early dawn.
Take a whirl on the waltz-around…
Go for an energetic wet kiss;
And, spend a memorable moment in nature's amorous armpit.

3.5 Culture Breathes Life unto the Lifeless

Why pass the buck when you originated the game?
You blame me when marriage collapses.
Incriminate me when sex desire no longer unite.
Accuse me of your ill-heartedness.
Defile me, then call me an evil-filler.
I am the patsy of your choice.
I'm culture.

Culture's fountainhead of self-growth.
It fosters body-mind-soul refinement.
As, it reflects on who we're;
Where we've been; and,
What we hope to be.
For, when we genuinely breathe our culture,
Illusion 'n reality divorce.
As, love kisses the heavens.

Culture opens the sense of beauty:
It limits us not.
Rather, the vastness we do not enter does.
Infatuated by chains of hope 'n love,
It teaches:
Great men have faults.
As there's strength in weakness;
And, light in darkness.
For, one defines the other.
As culture breathes life unto the lifeless.

3.6 As the Wave Crashes

…As the wave crashes down…
Even though times were tough;
Humanity shone.

    …As the wave crashes down…
    Even though times are tough;
    Humanity shines.

        …As the wave crashes down…
        Even though times will be tough;
        Humanity will shine – again.

Chapter 4

Integrity

*There's nothing so delightful as the hearing,
Or the speaking of truth.
For this reason, there is no conversation so agreeable,
As that of the man of integrity,
Who hears without any intention to betray,
And speaks without any intention to deceive.*

~ Plato (424 - 348 BC) ~

4.1 Hate the Sin but Love the Sinner

Turnin' in the widenin' gyre,
The falcon can no longer hear the falconer.
As the centre's loosened courtesy of institutionalized religions.
Religions that infuse inane faith in high-doses,
Straight into the ignorant followers' veins.
Makin' them believe in absurdities.
For, they're based on 'truths' that are told with ill-intent.
Intent to confuse, colonize and enslave.

Wear integrity as your garment,
And, the wind shall tear no holes unto the house of your soul.
Make *your* religion less of a theory;
And, more of a love affair;
Through the path of fairness 'n compassion.
This will usher you into the spiritual realm:
The sphere of grace 'n celestial serenity.
As your religion becomes humanity.

Unquestioningly, He walks in the clouds 'n descends in rain.
He sings in insects 'n waves in trees.
Makin' religion 'n spirituality [as] concomitants,
As the action of a rosella parrot -
Who flies with wings *shut-beatin'-shut*.
Thence, spirituality without religion's sterile; and,
Religion without spirituality's infertile.
So, go ahead: Drink-a-beer 'n have-good-sex;
Smoke-a-joint 'n kill-war.
Throughout, feel good when you do good;
And, feel bad when you do bad.
Hate the sin but love the sinner.
And, live immaculately that death trembles to steal you.

4.2 Absence's the Highest Form of Presence

Life's a mask.
A mask through which nature expresses herself.
Nature's a hall for mask-dance:
With masks - we dance the heaven-dance.
As humor's the mask of wisdom;
And, mask reveals more than the masked-face.
O' three masks, we wear: One of who we're.
One of who we think we're 'n the one of who others think we're -
As we face the jaws of life.

Mask distempers pride on the face,
With which to smash the venomous fangs of Universe.
Leavin' only the original pride.
Pride overlaid on earth-bound rib-bones.
In readiness for the hammers of changin' years;
For the sleepin' years of silence;
And, for the challengin' years of sunfire.
As mask freshens the face with sunrays.
Like a proud-eyed gambler - waitin' for the sunrise.
Removed thus, the kingdom's stolen.

Mask masks the true essence of purity.
Sealed with elemental chemicals of maternity.
Behold the masked beauty: Suave 'n voluptuous lips;
Lithe 'n sinuous soma…
Is a divine concinnity married to strength divine.
Whose ecstasies of arrant stateliness give deities a pause.
Sculpted by miraculous palms.
To charm the happy leisure of the goddess of elegance.
For, absence's the highest form of presence;
And, presence's the highest form of absence.

4.3 Presence's the Highest form of Absence

[As the first tale perused 'n laid;
A second to you, I opposite turn.
As life's a mask.]

As a traveller of thoughts 'n years –
Of youth long sped 'n middle-age declinin' -,
I hear the podcaster podcast: *Let's dance!*
Dance the dance of masks.
A dance in-which e'ery mask's perfect.
As e'ery mask's a real face;
And e'ery face's a real mask.
For, the face has reincarnated into multi-selves,
Of variegated deformities.
Birthin' a mask with neither face nor name…
A thingy with neither fore nor rear.
But, the swollen veins at the temples,
Betray the raw strain of peccancy.

> O' the masked man!
> He who's afraid of light.
> For, diabolical darkness looms beneath his gloomy mask.
> Hidden in the darkroom of his egoic thoughts.
> Born-of theatrical theatre of his excessive Art;
> For, self-servin' entertainment(s).
> O' treachery unique!
> Turns at the top into a malformed double-visaged freak.
> Abysmally lighted by a direful grimace that intoxicates all.
> A thingy with neither fore nor rear –
> Faceless, nameless 'n shameless.

> > O' reader of charm!
> > Your mind's a great ocean.

Pursue her secret deepness 'n impregnate self with
mindfulness;
Not be afraid of your journey of nobility.
Revolve, thus, not on the Universe of shallowness…
Instead, play upon the fountain of purity 'n
beatitude.
Beyond the dyin' essence of this mask of darkness.
E'en to the finish, dumped among the used-up
cinders,
This mask, (wo)men of good should say,
is fresh 'n flash.
For, in 'n with it:
Absence's the highest form of presence;
And, presence's the highest form of absence.

Notes on the poems

Absence and presence form consciousness. Thus, if there is absence there is presence to know the absence. Similarly, if there is presence there is absence to validate the presence. This is the essence of the Ying-Yang duality.

Chapter 5

Resilience

*You may be always victorious,
If you will never enter into any contest,
Where the issue does not wholly depend upon yourself.*

~ Epictetus (50 - 135 AD) ~

5.1 You are the Captain of Your Soul

The joy of life's in livin' it.
In courageously facin' odds;
And, in sweetenin' the desolate spots.
For the soil's richer than when the toil began.
The joy of life's soothin' our souls with heartily laughs;
'Til our visions are as vivid as a stream flow.
In dreamin' splendid dreams;
'Til our life-wagons hitch to the Sun.
For, joy of livin' is in soarin' in life.

Like the eagle of the sky,
Believe in your majestic wings.
Feel the wind caressin' your able wings,
Ascendin' effortlessly heavenward.
It matters not how strait the path is;
Nor how charged the scroll is:
You're the captain of your soul.
So, ne'er quit dreamin'; and,
Ne'er let love depart from your heart.

O' dear your wings are sure 'n strong.
And, the Universe ne'er ask us to bear,
That we can't soar o'er.
Thence, fret not on the life's twists 'n turns.
Rather, keep faith with a singleness of aim.
For, only today's yours to claim.
So, breathe happiness - live happiness.
As soar, you must…
May the wind under your wings bear you,
Where the Sun sails 'n the Moon marches.

5.2 Soar with Eagles and Roam with Mustangs

A cackle's heard, a shriek undone.
Encroachin' melancholy like a tornado elated to havoc.
Feel like endless drillin' the canyons of your soul;
Sensation like sailin' upstream with sails of death sound.
A silence sound so loud that,
You can't discern: Which way's bottom, which way's top.
As senses are dulled: No hearin', no feelin', no seein'…
Answers dim while questions throng.

Life isn't about prayin' for the storm to slip…
It's about learnin' to dance in the hail;
And, becomin' a storm unto self.
That's what the storms of life are all about.
As pleasure's at times born of pain.
A precious gain that takes you,
For a delightful ride through the sky…
To the pure-most lotus in the paradisiacal pond.

O' dear you know, as I do:
The implacable Sun stops not,
When obscured by dark, pernicious clouds;
And, gaiety rides storm waves.
So, be the calm eye of the storm;
Focus on your centre 'n remain calm.
Let your life flow like a stream of wind.
And, soar with eagles 'n roam wild with mustangs.
So, with infinite fuel to enliven,
I offer you: A calmin' lamp to lend a sight…
I whisper to you: Let me sprinkle flamboyance on your cheeks…
…Kiss away the beads of pain from your forehead.

5.3 Be a Bamboo that Stoops but Never Snaps

I dreamt past 'n future dreams.
Dreams of a mythical 'n cosmic friend.
A friend who like the air pervades everythin'.
Dreamt of a Queen with a heart as invigoratin' as the moonlight;
A soul as virgin as uncontaminated snow;
And, eyes as fair as the ocean blue.

> You're the stars 'n the rollin' thunder,
> You deserve love the depth of the ocean,
> Higher than imaginable heights.
> Each second with you,
> I fall deeper into you;
> Into love that holds-on 'n let go not.
> Your heart-warmin' laughter 'n contentin' cheers,
> Will ne'er be taken for granted.
> And, you'll ne'er travel life without a witness…

> > I wish you to be a bamboo.
> > A bamboo that stoops but ne'er snaps.
> > Keep calm 'n free yourself to sway.
> > Gently dance to the rhythm of the winds;
> > But, firmly stand to the ground.
> > Embrace the lows to make the highs sweeter.
> > All upheld by the truth that you're not entirely perfect.

5.4 Embodiment of Perfection

Fetid formless *'cancer'* is a thief.
A pilfer that robs blindly with no remorse;
A soulless shapeshifter that stains life.
A heartless beast of the night;
That burns what it touches,
With no care for the innocent, and
No mercy for the good.
But, ne'er cripples authentic love.

O' friend, in your soul, I know purity rarely seen.
An embodiment of perfection.
No artist's pallet can conspire.
This is the colour, this savage can steal not.
You'll be okay as we need you to be.
You'll be fine;
For, the Universe needs your effortless grace 'n elegance.
So, keep feedin' the beat in your heart.
And, let not this beast corrode your faith.

Don your armour - raise your sword,
And, win this foreign battle.
Show neither faint heart nor weak intent.
As we're all rootin' for you.
Formin' a circle of memory:
With neither beginning nor end.
For, yesterday's history;
Tomorrow a mystery; and,
Today a gift, thence called: present.
Relish the present;
And, let not this brute shatter your hope.

5.5 Universe in Ecstatic Motion

I know of an artist:
A fierce artist.
An artist who illustrates with fierce alacrity.
From life to integrity;
From love to humility;
From hope to femininity…
She lays all with charismatic clarity.
Immortalizing thoughts 'n their untold worth.
I know a fierce artist:
An epitome of elegance 'n refinement.
A woman who thinks quietly 'n acts frankly.
A lady who listens to stars 'n sages.
A dame who moves fluidly 'n steadily.
A fierce artist - a symphony of the Sky.

O' dear, meet all at the door with a smile
For, they're messengers sent from beyond.
Look at the sky not in the lake –
To see the real moon.
Keep diggin' your well…
Laugh as much as you breathe…
Dance not to the noise of bamboozlement…
Via the rays of your soul's light,
See the Deity gazin' at you from the mirror.
Walk boldly towards her path of love.
Like the Sun of *Njohi* – shine.
Like the Star of *Bicho* – shine.
Like the owner of Cosmos – shine.
For, you are the universe in ecstatic motion.

Dearest lovely one,

Keep unfoldin' your myth - unapologetically.
Move within but never in the way of fear.
Keep walkin' e'en when nowhere to walk to.
Feel both darkness 'n light within self.
Be the sky.
Live not with mice 'n spare self from cat claws.
Sell fishhooks nomore 'n be free-swimmin' fish.
Make a difference with each breath.
Be an eagle.
Dine less with nightingales 'n peacocks.
The former's mere a voice, the later just color.
Listen to self 'n let your journey unfold into an examined life.
Be a river of love 'n hope.

5.6 Achievement: A Signal to Grow

Achievement's a signal to grow 'n glow.
For, when the awareness of the achievable brushes our senses,
Our journey commences.
Credit belongs to those in the arena.
It belongs to those who strive valiantly; and,
Those who spend selves in a worthy cause.

> Recognition accords you an opportunity to spread wings.
> To put your heart into devotion with a smile.
> Throughout, give the world the best you have,
> And, the best will come unto you.
> Thence, conquer with dignity;
> Serve with love 'n soar with wit;
> And, you're destined to hit it big.

>> Your persistent determination fuels the hope forward;
>> Buildin' a momentum to successes.
>> You're perfect doers 'n exemplars of dedication.
>> A great people who look for solutions.
>> Make your achievement your benchmark.
>> Aim higher 'n not a single effort will be in vain.
>> For, happiness is in the thrill of creative effort.
>> So, keep your positive attitude alive 'n your enthusiasm aroused.

5.7 Want to Drench in Light

From the beginnin' my spirit was up;
While my thoughts overflowed with hope.
With honour 'n unbowed:
Up 'n down I roved – Africa-America-Asia-Europe…
Like a shadow, questions followed:
Not always visible 'n yet omnipresent.
Wearin' out the soul 'n exited naked 'n dreadful.
But, with honour 'n unbowed:
Up 'n down I roved –
From street to street with a disjointed mind…
For, Law seemed to be the wisdom not of the old.

E'eryone enjoys a fair contest.
But, this competition was savagely fierce:
Three thousand-nine hundred 'n ninety one interested;
Only two hundred selected.
Selected - I was…
And, I confess:
Slice of my life's achievements'
A fruit of bare-knuckle fights.
For the table was tilted from conception…
The game was rigged at inception…
But today, I want to self-drown.
I want to soak in knowledge.
I want to drench in light.
As Law's the sense of the young.

O' yeah!
I want to bed books that show me how to see.
I want voices that teach me new words to describe
love.

I want teachings that (re)kindle fires in my soul.
I want percepts that'll keep my flame burnin' in
different beautiful ways.
As I rove up 'n down the deep valleys of life,
With an enlightened mind…
…So, I'm goin'…
Goin' to wed Law;
As Law's good mornin' 'n good night.

I end this Chapter by sharing a lesson from one of my favourite poet - Thomas Hardy (1840 – 1928). Hardy (1994: 13) tells us:

> Every child is musical. Unfortunately this natural gift is squelched before it has time to develop. From all my life experience I remember being kicked out of school choir at because my voice and the words I sang did not please someone. My second-grade teacher, Miss Stone, would not let me sing with the rest of the class because she judged my voice as not musical and she said I threw the class off key. I believed her, which led to the blockage of my appreciation of music and blocked my ability to write poetry.
>
> Fortunately, at the age of fifty-seven (57) I had significant emotional event, which unblocked my ability to compose poetry. Poetry, which many people believe has lyrical qualities.

I hope reading this Chapter will take the place for you a significant emotional event and awaken your inner-self.

Chapter 6

Love

True love has no happy ending.
For, there is no ending to true love.

~ Alexander the Great (365 – 323 BC) ~

6.1 Love Reveals the Way of Light

Zeno of Elea (495-425 BC) posits:
The wheel that squeaks loudest gets greased.
And, if you wish to change a child,
Examine self-first…
For, you might be the one in need of a fix.
These thoughts might sound unromantic,
But, handled by the headstrong 'n impetuous,
Humanism's a Dutch-oven.
A cocotte of confusion that is stirred constantly.
Shouts are responded to with shouts.
As trumpetin' self-righteousness becomes ubiquitous.
- Quasi metaphorical pyromaniac -
It flushes away optimism;
And, extinguishes flicker of hope - antithema to real love!

Authentic love's divine 'n timeless.
'Tis inspired by reverence for unearthliness,
And, a profound predilection for winsome Zen.
Its precepts e'er eloquent 'n fair;
Hallmarked by deep consternation pulsatin' altruistic feelings.
Callin' us to solemnly apply our plumbs 'n squares,
To shape a glorious one…
As night fades to the dawn of deliverance;
And, trees bow to the winds of our aura.

So, let's go of the heavy iron chains of unrefined ego.
Shed-off the rusted links that tie you to Osiris.
For, emergin' from the broken chrysalis,
Is a butterfly of elegance 'n grace.
And, through genuine love, we reveal the way of light.

6.2 Be the Pillar of Flame in the Storm of Life

O'er a quarter of a Century today,
In one, by twos 'n threes, youngsters concenterin',
Walked the paths to learn how to chase ignorance.
The intention: perfect 'n divine.
Whene'er one uttered turbulent words;
Sisterhood whispered: forgive 'n forget.
Whene'er one experienced interior vistas,
Of phantasmic tongues that lick lambent tableaux;
Brotherhood purred: inner-peace.
Sister/brotherhood murmured: our joint fortune must flow in unison.
In a uni-channel like torrents' rush from a snow-mountain,
Mingled in peace through the valleys down.
For, beauty conquers ugliness 'n love conquers hate.

O' sensuous 'n compassionate sisters,
Lovers of fairness,
I offer you these lines with brotherly affection.
I dare say: A sister's a gift to the heart 'n a boon to the spirit,
She's the golden thread to the meanin' of life.
As she only giggles when one tells tales.
For, she instinctively knows where decorations have been added.
She points-out what the world's too polite to mention.
For, a sister's love's both unconditional 'n unbendable.

O' brothers, I bring to fore a hidden treasure.
To bridge an ocean-wide gap 'n tribute to your brotherly kindness.
A tribute to brothers who fill each other's life with a rush-of-energy.
I say thus: It takes two men to make a brother.

For, where there's no tie that binds, men are merely lined-up.
A true brother calms his brother's fears 'n wipes his tears.
A brother pillars his brother; and,
Ne'er let him wander in darkness singly.
As, love for 'n from a brother's irreplaceable.

All's done 'n finished in the celestial sphere.
But, flowers of intentions are kept eternally fresh by love.
Let's fly with each other with the elegance of a dove.
For, when you help your sister/brother's boat across,
Yours reach the shore too.
So, let's singly 'n cumulatively seek light in the darkest moments.
And, be the pillar of flame in the storm of life.

6.3 Seed of a Fresh Foundation

Why did he chose this spinose form?
- I hear you ask -
I asked him the same…
And, he retorted:
I'm the desert survivor,
Might not be as pretty as my cousin rose.
But with beauty, she sacrifices her life;
While I live for decades.
For, the desert has made me strong 'n wise.

> Most are quick to judge;
> For they see thorns not flowers.
> I saw both in the desert's heir.
> So, I dared offer you the misconstrued cactus…
> Instead of tulips.
> For, cactus' full of humility, but ne'er passive.
> As it epitomizes hard 'n soft;
> Toughness 'n tenderness.
> I dared offer you the misapprehended cactus…
> Instead of a rose.
> For cactus die not.

>> Step back 'n let it amaze you;
>> Don't go too far though as 'til need you.
>> Give it a fertile ground 'n water it.
>> Shine upon it with rays of love; and,
>> Propagate your full expression…
>> Throughout,
>> Listen to the silence – it speaks;
>> Listen to your heart – it knows.
>> Like a cactus in the desert.

6.4 Come Back: Above the Clouds - Below the Stars

Love starts as a feelin' but to continue's a choice.
I chose you e'ery sunup - despite my failings.
Imperfect I remain - like a pulpit;
Saintly furnished, but, dull in places unkissed by light.
A fact exaggerated now by our seemingly unaligned stars.
These lines thence,
Serve as a monument to a string of moments once dear.
A survivin' testament to a time…
A time when our amorous bridges were unwrapped;
Before they turned unsweet rubble.

Buried in this selfish miscomprehension:
All thoughts are lifeless.
Concealed in this loathly loneliness:
Beauty's smoked 'n life gives-in.
Trapped in this dark cage of strength:
Senses are strangled divorcin' one from self-wisdom.
Robbed - one feels – but, unsure what has been thieved;
As ones memories are distorted.

Tears run blood in my veins.
I close eyes 'n hope for you.
For, I ne'er imagined a life-less-you.
All I want is you to come back to life.
As behind these darkened lifeless walls;
Lies a boundless shinny Universe,
A lovely world where goodliness lurks – like before.
Only if you dare look 'n listen;
Forge ahead 'n face fear head-on.

6.5 Beauty no Picture can Picture

Love begins as a feelin', but to continue's a choice.
I choose you e'ery sunrise.
For, in your cinematic eyes, I discovered a night-sky full of stars.
In your laughter, I unearthed a godly symphony.
Unified thus, we remain the light.
The light at the end of this endless life-tunnel - for each other.

Like a candle, you burn inside my soul,
Guidin' me through life-hiccups.
As like a handprint on cement –
An indelible heartily mark - you left.
Bendin' my identity,
At the meet-point of your kind 'n tender fingers.
Above the clouds - below the stars thence;
Come-back 'n re-find the colours.
Polychromatic colours we together dreamt-of.

Let's, again, love like the spark betwixt flint 'n stone.
Love in reckless abandonment,
Promisin', upon each dawn:
To choose a thing to re-love in each other.
To your goodself, I submit:
Dayspring can't get stale…
Fire of love can't be tamed…
Love lyrics can ne'er be nails on a boardwalk;
For, the bridge betwixt us' heavenly.
And, you're a beauty no picture can picture.

6.6 Love's Sufficient Unto Love

Love gives naught but itself.
Love takes naught but from itself.
Love neither possesses nor can it be possessed.
For, love's infinite.
So, why: I-Love-You?
A misunderstood, over-used 'n ab-used phrase.
A phrase capturin' mechanical feels towards the 'other'.
'I-Love-You' killed love.
To un-kill love, I settle for:
I think you - I breathe you;
I taste you - I feel you...

> O' sweetly, you deserve love to the infinite - the best.
> As you're the best.
> In your eyes, I see the beauty of a clear-sky,
> While your heart shines the love I love to sight.
> Your life oxygenates my World;
> While, your World waters my life.
> You're the catalyst for my soul's betterment.
> Thus, I cite you to justify [my] inner-peace,
> And, put your heart as guarantor on [my] life.
> So, I say: I dream you - you complete me…

>> Love's mechanical not.
>> For, love's sufficient unto love: infinite.
>> True love's conferred with magnanimity.
>> Pure love looks not to convenience.
>> Real love's steadfast 'n unaltered by temporal vicissitudes.
>> So dear, let's make love-for-the-other an action of care 'n hope,

Inspired by inner sense 'n gentle touch of the 'other's' soul.

6.7 Trickling Sap of Ki-Family

This hour, I go confidence.
I'm no prouder than my pen.
I trouble so, not my soul to vindicate [it]self.
For, elementary laws apologize not.
But, I confess: I wanted to unscrew the locks from the doors.
Wanted to unscrew the doors from their jambs.
But, I question not the reality.
As, I believe in appetites: tastin' 'n smellin'.
Seein', hearin' 'n feelin' are other daily miracles.
And, a morning-glory satisfies –
More than the metaphysics of books.
So, I waited for you atop Tacoma.

I waited 'n witnessed atop Tacoma.
With e'ery ticklin' second pacin' into hours - I began to rave.
Drownin' in the sea of passin' faces,
I faxed my care 'n kisses – your way.
Hummin' for ultimate surprise: Your appearance.
Accompanied with the moon - you appeared.
I felt my inspiration 'n respiration.
I tasted the smoke of my breath.
I heard the throbs of blood in my arteries;
And, the flashes of air through my lungs.
As my words dissolved in the eddies of the wind.

Here comes the touch of my lips to yours –
The murmur of yearnin'.
Here comes the height of reflection - the pleasures of heaven.
The sea breathin' broad 'n convulsive breaths – 'tis you!
Sun so generous – 'tis you!
Vapours lightin' inner-me – 'tis you!

Most certain sure - plumb in the uprights – 'tis you!
Breast that kisses my breasts – 'tis you!
Nest of guarded duplicate eggs – 'tis you!
Tricklin' sap of Ki-family – 'tis you!
Mortal touched to be touched – 'tis you.
For, my voice goes for what my eyesight can touch not.
…I believe in you - my light…

6.8 The Ring of Life

I searched pristine ridges 'n pure dales…
Finally, I found life's truest beauty:
Soft sunsets 'n colorful rainbows;
Silent moments 'n a supernal her.
Settin' my mind free.
Free to dream skyward.
To dream the dream of happiness.
Dream of dreams.
Though this dream's path's calm 'n secure
My footin' feels unsure – *sans elle*.

O' dear, you deserve the very best.
You deserve:
Love deeper than the ocean 'n higher than mountains;
Love brighter than the sun 'n refreshin' than rainwater.
You deserve:
Love that lets you glow 'n grow boundlessly;
Love that lets you mould 'n live your dream(s).
That's the love I guarantee you –
Through this Ring of Life.

This Ring I offer you, is a piece of my soul.
This Ring I offer you, is an exemplar of my inner intentions:
To stand by you;
To swim through the waves of life with you – now 'n fore'er…
For this Ring, is a piece of my heart.
With this Ring thus, I ask you to be the moon in my light.
Through this Ring, I ask you to be the day to my night.
With this Ring, I ask you to be the *Ying* to my *Yang*.
Through 'n with this Ring…
I ask you to be my heart 'n make me complete.

I ask you to wrap me up in you;
And, let my happiness be yours 'n your sadness mine.
By acceptin' this Ring – my soul, my heart.

This Ring I offer you - today,
Epitomizes what I smell-see-feel-taste-hear in us…
In us: I smell a thousand future holds.
In us: I see sunup 'n moon-beam delight;
I see the sweetest design unravel.
In us: I taste the goodies outta the Universe.
In us: I hear the Ocean make her wishes.
In us: I touch unadulterated love.
I smell-see-feel-taste-hear (all) this through your eyes.
Eyes whose sparkles match the stars in a moonless sky.

6.9 Kingston Song

Kingston song…
A song of tender fire.
Fire of love on a raging sea.
Powerful and deep to weather life storms.
With hearts so pure 'n love so sweet.

>Kingston song…
>A song of tender heat.
>Heat of love that makes hearts fly on gossamer wings –
>Through cloudless skies.
>For, it sees with the soul;
>Making reality better than dreams.

>>Kingston song…
>>A song of breeze.
>>Breeze of pristine air –
>>Through flowerin' forests of roses.
>>As it smells the smell of refined love:
>>So sweet 'n pure.

Chapter 7

Hope

Hope is a waking dream.

~Aristotle (384 – 322 BC) ~

7.1 Dealer in Hope

Dearest friend…,
Thank you for being you:
Sociable;
Remarkable;
Dependable;
Indefatigable;
And, knowledgeable.

You've shown what great leadership's about.
Ne'er blowin' uncertain trumpets.
Rather, you listen with curiosity;
Speak with honesty; and,
Act with integrity.
For, like a candle,
You consume yourself to light the way for others.

You're an authentic guidin' light - an inspiration.
Ne'er hesitant to share your wisdom; and,
Ne'er reluctant to empower.
I only hope you know.
That you're an exemplar of humility.
With untainted vision, you elevate those around you.
With a refined spirit, you enrich all.
Kind 'n gentle, you remain.
For, nothing's so strong as gentle;
Nothing's so gentle as real-strength.
So, a true dealer in hope – you're.
Profferin' me a reason,
To be thankful about.

7.2 Path to Tranquillity Passes Through Storms

Oftentimes, life forces us to walk un-trailed paths -
Uphill through dazzlin' daze 'til dark-clouds' wrath.
'Til darkness blinds our eyes 'n swims into our ears.
Keepin' us from seein' light 'n hearin' joy.
Lines get blurred 'n colours are no longer vibrant.
No more beauty in the sunset 'n no majesty in the sea.
The sound of laughter gets more bitter than sweet;
And, e'ery song's the same bleak susurrus.
A kiss reminds us nothing good lasts;
While other interactions make the skin crawl.
Ultimately, the brewin' storm breaks us…

O' reader, run not from the storm - storm into it.
For, once broken-open, we unearth what's inside us.
We (re-)discover our true beauty 'n our real strength.
Stomp into it, as, you're lightnin' made flesh:
Unstoppable as the desert sands ridin' the wind; and,
E'ery Sun breaks 'n e'ery storm falters.
And, the path to tranquillity passes through storms.
Crucially, walk-out of the storm a warrior not a victim.

O' yeah, if you know nothing,
Know that you're not alone.
That, I've your back no matter what…
Keep in mind: The storm will pass;
The hurt will heal 'n the burden shall be repaid.
Just keep pressin' beyond self-delightful assurance.
And, with your divine smile,
Flowers will again utter cries of felicity;
And, the Deity of light will unveil unseen heavens.

7.3 Constant Source of Hope

The mask took form;
Revealin' the innocence of eyes.
Eyes that appeared softly wild - no sign of vile.
But, their deeds - full of manipulation;
While their words served as abominable stimulation.
As, they abhorred your dreamin';
And, wanted less profound you.
They expected you to be like a pigeon's passive waddle –
To their scattered tidbits.
For, they enjoyed you floatin'.
Floatin' in their streams of toxic imaginations
Not-for-long!

> Hear the flutterin' of your feathers,
> Swoopin' down to night-time perch.
> Incitin' a melody of glory from your soul at nature's worth.
> Feel joy creep to the innermost contentment of your heart.
> A heart of gold that bears silent witness:
> Enchanted eyewitness.
> You're a livin' testimony of resilience.
> An exemplar of the power of believin' in self.

>> Go forth to where beauty lies.
>> Counsel truly filled with light.
>> Overfilled with words that mend a punctured heart;
>> And, soothe a wounded soul.
>> So, like a candle with a far off-flame:
>> Faintly re-glow.
>> As you follow your golden elegance of universal dimensions.

Exquisiteness marked by a curvature of manifold directions.
Through your shared light,
Feel the sky reveal, a rainbow adornin' so divine.
For, a constant source of hope 'n a true anchor you're.

7.4 We can make the World Beautiful

A pitcher cries for water to carry;
A person for joyous work -
For a respite however brief!
As when we work we're a flute…
A flute through whose heart,
The whisperin' of the hours turns musical.
Bringin' us intimate with life's innards.
So, with the heavens above my head,
And earth beneath my feet;
I want to breathe the breath.
The breath of the primrose sweet…
I want to feel as I used to feel;
Before I knew the walk that earns a meal!

I want to breathe – again.
Want to feel as I used to feel - again.
So, I join a people…
Join a people who pulls the cart with patience;
A people who strain in the muck to move things forward.
A people who submerge in the harvest;
Passin' the bags rhythmically 'n joyfully;
Even if the 'Other' shall enjoy the harvest.

In the wakefulness of noontide, I say thus:
The world could be [more] beautiful…
For e'ery teardrop hinders needle 'n thread.
In the wakefulness of noontide, I reiterate:
The wind speaks not more sweetly to the giant oaks,
Than to the blades of grass.
And, great's who turns the voice of the wind into a melody.
A melody made sweeter by one's own lovin'.

***

Collectively thence, let's sow seeds with tenderness,
   E'en if the 'Other' shall to enjoy the harvest.

Chapter 8

Fairness

I have nothing to ask,
But that you would move to the other side.
That you may not,
By intercepting the sunshine,
Take from me what you cannot give.
Stand a little less between me and the Sun.

~ Diogenes (404 – 323 BC) ~

8.1 Cherish Fairness and Justice

Beings cherish fairness 'n justice.
Thence, obliviousness to the aspirations of the other;
As we egoically pursue self-success;
Is morally repugnant 'n pragmatically revoltin'.
None-the-less, eulogies continue;
To resound in stentorian tones.
For, the self-infatuated know-it-all...

What of the humble man, *sans* societal perch?
The man who receives collective shallow acts when all he wish for is fairness.
He's twisted in circles by two-faced heartless truth-twisters.
Twisters with hatred in their veins.
That waters the seeds of life with acrid acid.
As in their presence, fairness loses meanin';
And, foulness becomes the reignin' queen.
Fluent with the concepts of death,
Whate'er they set eyes on, attains a warped beauty,
E'en the deity of evil greatly envies them.

Let not these truth-benders tame your innate wilderness:
Raise your soul 'n smell the wild breeze of futurity.
Be the Sun on flooded field 'n the fire for tangled web.
For, 'tis better to be with a handful of good men fightin' the bad;
Than be with hosts of bad men fightin' a handful of good.
And, 'tis wiser to fall-in with crows than with flatterers;
For, with the former, you're devoured only when dead;
But, with the latter while alive.
So, be brave 'n kiss their hatred with an angelic tongue;
And, show 'em how to shine – fair 'n just.

8.2 Fairness is in Action

Light must be painful to night!
With a pretentious smile, the truth-fiddlers bend honeyed words.
Words that mask their inherent bile.
With their lips stained with fresh blood of their last kill,
They lurk, wait 'til you're most vulnerable.
Close-in 'n devour you – inside-out.
'Til you can hear the Sun no more.
[I've been there – lately…]

These truth- twiddlers are like a king.
A king who wanders his kingdom lookin' for the king.
For, half their livers are swollen with egotism;
The other half with hypocrisy.
Thus, they're drunk 'n driven by the spirits of hatred.
In the midst of their theatre of hatred towards the 'other',
My smile hid the scars in the soul.
I declare thence: this is a battle tween crooked grins of mischief,
And, vicious destructive forces of ill-will.

Dear reader, live fairness, profess it not.
For, fairness' in action, not in wording.
Seek 'n leave jollity in e'ery path you tread;
Make others feel that there's something in them.
So, think only the best, work only for the best,
And, expect only the best.
Be as enthusiastic about the success of the 'other',
As you're about yours.
Give so much time to self-improvement,
That you've no time to hate.
Be a greater human being;
And, the world will be more equal 'n fair.

8.3 The Way of Fairness is My Life's Purpose

To unearth the butterfly of elegance 'n grace...
To really know the thrill of health, a man must first be ill.
Similarly, he who has oppression felt 'n conquered;
'Tis he who really knows the happiness of being free.
For, the only happy time of rest's that which follows strife;
...And see some contribution unto the joy of life.
So, like a finisher, I finish...
By valorously turnin' the unturned 'n sayin' the unsaid.

> Ne'er will their stone wrought hearts animate to life!
> In their drunkenness they predicted: The top will be the bottom;
> And, the bottom will dive into the ocean-bottom.
> What a myopic illusion!
> I dined 'n danced with crabs' king,
> Clickin' castanets than ne'er before.
> For, 'tis unwise to teach a swine how to sing.

>> O' unwisers, you can take air away from me - if you wish,
>> But, you'll ne'er dim the light from within.
>> As I follow the glow of distant light,
>> Away from your hate-full arena.
>> So, with a logic of indisputability,
>> I refuse to be a piece to your moronic puzzle.
>> Like unbowed Pollyanna who tastes hate to arouse love thus,
>> Away, I decidedly slither-off your
>> chokin' cave of darkness...
>> A cave of staleness...
>> A cave devoid of past, present or future...

To the faithful lamp of the unhurried,
With indescribable feelin' of pure serenity…
Avowin' solemnly 'n unapologetically:
The way of fairness is my life's purpose!

Chapter 9

Humility

*Nothing is softer than water.
Nothing more flexible than water.
Yet nothing can resist it.*

~ Lao Tzu (571 – 447 BC) ~

9.1 We Descend to Rise

The greatest wisdom's in knowin',
That we know nothing.
For, there's no birth of consciousness without pain.
We were born stumblers;
And, life's beauty's in the stumblin'.
Ergo, like a tower that pierces the clouds,
We must descend to rise.
And, the higher the structure,
The deeper it must go.
Humbled by its under-structure:
Unshakeable foundation.

Discard omnipotence tendencies,
And, emerge from the dreams of omniscience.
Accept not your dog's admiration,
As conclusive evidence of your infallibility.
Rather, think deeply of the world 'n lightly of self.
For, nothing's more distasteful,
Than takin' the path that leads to self.

Arrogance has nothing to do with greatness.
It corrodes righteousness 'n in its presence,
The existence of virtue's a staged appearance.
At the sight of potential for mastery thus,
Be like the egoless ocean - streams bow to her.
They willingly flow into her as she's lower.
For, her humility accords her power.
Similarly, keep-off from the greatness that bows not to the low;
And, reveal your heavenly lights.
As we near greatness when we're great in humility.

9.2 Humility Disarms Self-centeredness

Heraclitus (535 -475 BC) taught me:
He who tries to arrogantly shine, dims his light.
For, pride repels while humility inspires.
Engrossed in this lesson 'n with folded arms on my windowsill,
I gaze at Titicaca's starlit sky so still.
Amidst the awe of a pellucid wonder, I ponder:
When the wintery wind arrives, it lays bare the oaks.
Gone are the leaves of deeds that bear thoughts of pride.
Thence, if these trees were saints who ejaculate truth,
Humanity would be a withered tree with wilted leaves!
Humbled by nature.

O' humanity, know the seed before the nascence.
Let it reveal from deep within...
Enablin' compassion to sprout wings - in your cradle.
Let humility soar from thoughts akin...
Allowin' integrity to shine forth from the rubble.

Let humility radiate from within 'n say:
Fortuitous spider, I bow to your song...
Blade of summer grass, teach me...
For, humility disarms self-centeredness 'n greediness.
It dissolves swell-headedness 'n unwarm-heartedness.
As greater love hears itself:
The higher it grows,
The deeper it bows.

9.3 Paint Your Life with Humility

Be the…
The humility.
Humility that shines from within 'n without.
Humility that thrusts you into ethereal forbearance.
For, you're the ethereal forbearance lavishin' a merciful grace.
Grace upheld by the oozin' charm.
So be the…

>Be the…
>Be the grace.
>The grace upheld by fluency;
>And, over-exuberance of a humble kind.
>The like of an ancient baobab-tree born from a tiny seed;
>Yet, gives love in perpetuity.
>Shine your life with the humility of the rainbow;
>And, boundless greatness will attend you.
>So, be the…

>>Be the…
>>Be the morning song sung by the birds of the air.
>>Be the chime of the gentle beasts of the ground.
>>Be the bubblin' of the stream windin' through a dense forest.
>>Be the spectacular auroras of dazzlin' northern lights.
>>Be the…

9.4 A Cup must be Empty to be Filled

A dwarf sittin' on giants' shoulders, I am.
I see that's more distant, not because of a superior sight,
But because your great statures add to mine.
As I stand on the shoulders of Giants: You!

My admiration for you is pure in its truth.
Your immortal souls beget seraphic imprints,
That my pen can hardly blazon forth.
For your veils are of unfeigned flowers.
Whose workmanship Deity adores.
I praise the saccharine-smell, which your aura forth cast;
There for honey-bees to sip-out strained nectar.
Whene'er I do my thing, I hear your melodious tunes;
Oozin' timeless sensuality, refined by time.
Tunes that remind me:
Nothing's more distasteful than takin' the path to self.
And, the humble side of life's far sunnier.
You teach me the language of beingness.
To which, I offer love in rhythm 'n of rhyme - a gift in form.

A cup must be empty to be filled.
To learn, one must unknow.
O' I confess: these ideas come *via* you.
For, your upliftin' commentaries reveal the unrevealed.
A perfect chisel to chip my imperfections, they offer.
To which I pledge:
My words shall fore'er be marked by unequivocal truth.
A sweet-scented promise that descends to your footsteps,
Direct from Aphrodite's altar bendin' with endearment.
So, abandon the fruitless cold virginity,
And, let your sheer presence dissipate the barbarous.

9.5 Humility: Origin of all things

Humility's the origin of all things.
It brightens dark roads;
And, levels rough roads.

> Humility blunts sharp edges.
> It softens glare;
> And, unties knots.

>> Humility's inexhaustible –
>> Once it exists.
>> 'Tis endless flow of energy.

Chapter 10

Nobility

A noble man emphasizes the good qualities in others.
He does not accentuate the bad.
The inferior does.

~ Confucius (551 - 479 BC) ~

10.1 Ideal Grace Secure from Taint of Time

Life's a game - played gamely.
Birthin' two genres of philanthropist:
Those who do little but make a great deal of babble;
Those who do a great deal but make no prattle.
Subscribe to the latter.
Uplift with no reason; and,
Give with no expectation.
And, be like the Parthenon Frieze - unsung song.
An ideal grace secure from taint of time.

Let your deportment remind all:
Harbourin' a noble idea makes us no noble.
Actin' on a noble idea makes us no noble.
Puttin' others before us makes us noble.
Thence, be the light that enables the other see.
Where the mind's bent upon an action kind;
Where the means are sparely spun;
Stretch them with compassion.
As we're called to nobility.

With love, I share a lesson from Sephora - my mother.
She taught me:
Good's ne'er so good;
As when you're unaware that you're doin' good.
You're ne'er so good;
As when you're unconscious that you're good.
For a saint's one, 'til he knows it!
And, the utmost heroism is not disrobin' your heroic deeds.
For, *une tigresse ne proclame jamais sa tigritude*.
Remain the tigress that you're.

10.2 Be Noble

Bush for the robin;
Air for the wing of the sparrow;
But, path to nobility's narrow.
As one can neither wrong 'n feel right,
Nor give pain 'n gain pleasure.
True worth is in being, not seemin';
In doing good, not in dreamin'.
For, nothing's kingly as kindness;
And, nothing's royal as truth.
Nothing's so sacred as honesty;
For, he who's honest is noble.

Nobility comes from fightin' besides your soldiers;
And, never from commandin' them.
For, a noble man enjoys not where he does not give joy.
Thus, nobility of spirit's about simplicity 'n wisdom.
'Tis about dedication 'n altruism.
As there's nothing noble in being superior to a fellow being.
True nobility's being meritorious to one's former self.
And, a noble soul isn't the one that manages the highest flights.
'Tis the one that rises very little 'n falls very little;
But ever dwells in a free 'n resplendent altitude.

Oft-time, the slope of life's slippery 'n tempestuous…
Compromised visibility 'n elusive tranquillity…
Nevertheless, toil well in the fields of life struggles,
That you reap nobler returns.
So, be noble;
And, the nobleness in others will meet thine own.

10.3 Nobility Journey

Three – born conjoined at hip.
Together - started a nobility journey.
Growin' up relyin' on brotherliness.
Stickin' together through the thick 'n the thin.
All that we did, we did together as young boys.
Knowin' that a win was always ours.

> Hillary was first to exit the journey…
> We took his departure pretty rough.
> We cried but our rivers dried-up.
> With only two left, our journey of nobility's raptured.
> 'Tis down to Dave 'n me wonderin' who's next to the door.

> The Saint of Darkness tires not.
> He punched on the clock;
> And, Dave Senior expired.
> Now, all alone –
> All I think of is my two twin-brothers gone.
> And how this all started out as nobility journey…
> A journey to be completed.

Chapter 11

Rest

Those who are skilled in archery,
Bend their bow only when they are preparing to use it.
When they do not require it,
They allow it to remain unbent.
For otherwise,
It would remain unserviceable when the time for using it arrived.

So, it is with man.
If he were to devote himself unceasingly to a dull round of business,
Without breaking the monotony by cheerful amusements,
He would fall imperceptibly into idiocy,
Or be struck by paralysis.

~ Herodotus (484 - 425 BC) ~

11.1 Embrace Glorious Lulls

Lyin' under a tree;
Listenin' to the murmur of the waters;
While watchin' the clouds float lazily across the sky:
Isn't indolence.
For, rest like silence has a sound - a fullness.
'Tis heavy with the sigh of a tree – space tween breaths.
'Tis ripe with pause betwixt birdsong - crash of surf.
'Tis a moment to consciously separate the past from the future.

Sacred rest 'n work are alterable symbols of the cosmos:
Permanence at rest 'n continuance in motion.
They symbolize dark 'n light strikin' each other -
Vividly etchin' colours of love through the horizon.
As there's virtue in work 'n rectitude in repose.

Overlook neither:
Hours for restfulness 'n hours for wakefulness;
Nights for sobriety 'n nights for drunkenness.
Find them in each other:
Activity in rest 'n rest in activity.
Find your *Lagrange Point* 'n be here 'n now,
With neither history nor future.
For, in life, nothing is e'er ended;
Everything only begin.

11.2 Rediscover Your Ground of being

Receive the world without judgment.
Quieten the stings of the prickin' conscience;
And, the incessant raucous clamour of unsatisfied soul.
Relish moments of tranquillity;
Enjoy a bath in the sea 'n a copious allowance of quality sex.
Indescribably serene 'n unhurried:
Turn-off the lights 'n perch in the dark.
Re-discover your ground of being;
And, arouse the natural liberation.
Liberation of your manifold self-identifications.

Embrace glorious lulls.
Lulls that have the quality of idyllic floatiness.
Floatiness borne-out of creative loafin'.
That carry the throb of being simultaneously too full,
And, too empty;
Evokin' discomfort of infinity.
Thus, live for happiness.

Seek peace in the inland murmur of streams,
And, the gracious wavin' of trees.
Seek harmony in the beauteous vesture of nature,
And, sublime pageantry of the skies.
Throughout, describe not…
Instead, be subject of description.

11.3 Posing in Silence

O' pleasure!
Pleasure posin' in silence - among the trees.
The immanence of nature's inherent harmony.
Posin' in the silence of delight:
An otherworldly specialisation;
A fresh pragmatic specialisation.
Posin' in silence.

>Fake friends pass roisterin' with power.
>Power of egotism 'n violence.
>No power's needed among the trees -
>Only truth 'n justice.
>No grievous ache's needed among the trees -
>Only a humble-purple stupefyin' aroma.
>Aroma that startles the sparrows.
>Posin' in silence.

>>O' unequalled pleasure of silence – among the trees.
>>Lilac coloured silence…
>>Regal in its resonance,
>>Of romance.
>>What's a pleasurable silence!
>>Gilded silence that flashes.
>>Frenzied silence that arouses.
>>Irresistible silence that soothes.
>>Split into fragments -
>>Fragments that remain intact.
>>Inexorably united with the infinite.
>>The infinite art of silence.
>>Unstoppable silence of silence.

Chapter 12

Dedication

*Until you spread your wings,
You'll have no idea how far you can fly.
For, you become strong by defying defeat.
And, by turning loss and failure into success.*

~ Napoleon Bonaparte (1769 – 1821 AD) ~

12.1 You can Steal not My Dream

Like a beast on its prey:
She lurks...
And waits, 'til you're most vulnerable.
Then closes-in 'n devours you – inside-out.
Leavin' a mere shell of you.
No more happiness,
No more love.
Total darkness.

At its peak,
She poured pure cold onto my soul.
I couldn't hear the Sun.
But, no one said life's fair.
So, I let her interrupt my dream.
Felt like a boilin' kettle.
But, the whistlin' tunes caressed my nerves.

O' you goddess of darkness!
You aimed at makin' me a walkin' marionette;
With torn strands.
But, I vowed:
I'll crumble not.
I'll stand;
I'll smile;
I'll love.
For, ne'er can you soil my dream.

12.2 Fire in Our Hearts

Full of ill 'n malignity...
The two's halfway spoken speech,
Breaks like a broken pledge.
Leavin' hopes blinded,
As they in unison pronounced:
No place for you on Earth –
You'll beat no more.
I softly responded: hold there, you jagged books...
Books of spite, heavy eye 'n gloomy mien...
For, I chanced to view an island.

The duo jagged books of spite taught me:
We have fire in our hearts.
Faced with grief grafted on old;
As the answerin' of thunder to thunder.
We have fire in our shinnin' souls.
Faced with noise of the 'two' piercin' eyes;
As the calling of sea unto sea.
We have in our hands the shinin'.

With the sorrowful bound unto sorrow -
I learnt to voice my pain.
As diversity was killed 'n I mourned for killed hope -
I grew a voice to cry my pain.
No more silent writhing in the dark...
No muttering of mute lips...
No caressing the knee-on-the-neck...
Ah, I-can-breathe!
O' yeah - at last,
I can drink Sun in the moonlight.
How it falls.

12.3 Have More to Think and Less to Say

Smellin' the sweetness of the high-fastidious night.
Awakenin' with the wise old stars.
Shinin' rich through the ruins of time.
And, loudly laughin' at the one who vows to the vulgar Sun;
Have more to think 'n less to say.

> Have less to say 'n more to think.
> For, you're the best version of self.
> Thus, resonate with your inner strength.
> Push your limits;
> And, expand your horizon.
> Evaluate your perception;
> Let self be silently drawn by the pull of what you love;
> And, find inner peace.
> Throughout, have more to think 'n less to say.

>> Have less to say 'n more to think;
>> And, see the sparkle that covers your being.
>> Recognize your essence of happiness;
>> And, awaken the dead sanctify of the bad soul.
>> (T)hencefore, enchant all that you sets sight on.
>> But, have more to think 'n less to say.

Chapter 13

Diversity

Variety is the spice of life.

~ African Proverb ~

13.1 Let Things be Different

In the last two decades in academia,
I have interacted with thousands of international souls.
Interacted with an interest of generatin' knowledge.
With some, we could agree not on what proceeds the other:
Day or night.
We could agree not whether a honeybee's black 'n yellow,
Or, yellow 'n black.
We could settle not on what was tasty.
Could find not a song that loved us both.
And, so I find a reason to sing:
Let things be different.

E'ery villain's a hero in his mind.
So, in the process of chasin' ignorance,
We sought non-generic answers.
We differed ideologically,
But, agreed that aggressive fight for conformity's raw delinquency.
As we were on a journey to see the beauty of divergence.
Thus, by makin' a difference in me,
You enabled me make a difference in you.
For, we ne'er learn from those who always agree with us.

Time goes not - we go;
Your locks are curled gold, while mine have shamed the crow.
In the selfsame stage,
We appreciate that life follows the *Ying-Yang* of nature.
Thence, we let things be different;
And, dance on the grey.
For, the nail that sticks-out farthest,
Doesn't necessarily need to be hammered the hardest.

13.2 Mutuality is the Best Creation

Aristotle (384-322 BC) notes:
Mutuality's the best creation.
I disagree not.
For, you polished me inside-out!
Meshed my brain;
Sawed together my nerve-endings;
And unclogged my blood-vessels.
Like a river of diamonds,
Shiny and pointed.

Baskin' in decent attitude 'n altitude.
For, you make me feel like a phoenix;
Feel like a skyscraper - of love 'n life.
Proudly swayin' 'n bendin' in the wind.
My adoration runs deep;
As we are connected by the soft breeze.

Caught in breezily moment in the startling azure sky;
My heart heads to Paris…
Caught atop fluffy squishy clouds floatin' lazily -
My head floats to Lyon…
I spread my wings 'n like an eagle high,
I bow my head.
And say:
Je suis ce que je suis ;
Grâce à ce que nous sommes tous!

13.3 *Ubuntu* Links Human Hearts

Ubuntu connects humanity.
It links human hearts in the web of life;
And, uncovers 'n discovers love.
From womb to tomb.

> Each to each returns its need.
> To respond to the other's call;
> And, become a full 'n active human being.
> Speak to the positive intent;
> And, bring-out the better side - of all.
> From womb to tomb.

>> Hear the cries of the 'other';
>> Clear obstacles from his path;
>> And, write a symphony in his voice.
>> Focus on interconnectedness;
>> And, boost the fortunate strokes.
>> Strokes of serendipity – for all.
>> From womb to tomb;
>> Let *Ubuntu* reign.
>> And say:
>> I am, because you are…
>> I am, because we are…

Notes for Poem 13.3

Ubuntu is a short form of *Umuntu Ngumuntu Ngabantu* in Zulu language. It means: *I am, because you are; and, since you are, I am.* The concept speaks to the fact that:
- There is oneness to humanity with connections invisible to the eye.
- One can only grow and progress through the growth and progression of others.
- We achieve ourselves by sharing ourselves with others.

Consequently, humanity is not a zero-sum game. Rather, it is a win-win set-up in which: one can be a victor without a victim and one can stand tall without standing on another person. There is therefore no need to tear the 'other' down to be up.

Chapter 14

Appreciation

*Taught by time,
My heart has learned to glow for other's good,
And, melt at other's woe.*

~ Homer (800 – 701 BC) ~

14.1 My Heart Melts

Dear readers,
Asante sana - hartelijk bedankt – grand merci...
Your personae are beyond belief.
For, your unified qualities, rare they're:
Compassionate 'n empathetic; considerate 'n angelic...
My heart melts in gratitude!

Caught in the intricate web of darkness,
In the distracted world of unmasked's chaos...
You listened, when most incoherent;
You picked, when in desolate shambles; and,
You paid, when e'en air was unreachable.
Now you say in unison: Ain't a big deal.
I say: It meant the world...
For, a soothing relief – you offered.
As, the greatest treasures are invisible to the naked eye,
But, felt by the heart.
My heart melts in appreciation!

...Many remain unlistened to - listen to 'em.
As we see pain with our ears; 'n hear its music with our eyes.
For, in the silence betwixt the notes, there lies the real-story.
...Many remain unpicked - pick 'em;
As the more we love, the more we're loved.
And, a candle loses no light by lightin' another candle.
...Many remain unpaid for - pay for 'em;
As our deeds are louder than our words.
And, there's more joy in givin' than in receivin'.
O' fellow citizens of humanity, uplift 'em all...
And, make their hearts melt in elation!

14.2 A Teacher-Magician-Butterfly…

Story telling's the art of being human-being.
It expresses our belief in morrow;
And, helps us feel the fragrance of goodness.
Goodness in the words used 'n the acts performed.
Leavin' us munificently perfumed.
Perfumed by the finest impulses that enable us decipher;
And, associate with words smithed by the master's strokes;
Like the tender shoots we tendered.
[T]hence, this' a story about a model:
Teacher-magician-butterfly…
'Tis about a being whose words chime…
Chime like the melodious bells of nirvana.
An earthlin' who makes the ordinary extraordinary;
And, the extraordinary ordinary.
A giver of hope to the hopeless 'n love to the unloved.

She teaches humanity by being the emblem of humanity.
As, fairness seeps from her synapses;
Equality spurts out of her arteries;
While, empathy [hall]marks her footsteps.
Her life teaches:
We aren't here to be small;
We aren't here to be perfect.
We're here to grow 'n glow;
We are here to learn 'n love.
We're here to catalyse the generative process of life.
By livin' for others as we live for ourselves.

She's a magician…
She taught me how to draw milk –
To draw milk from a mixture of milk 'n water;

She taught me how to get sugar –
To get sugar from a mixture of sugar 'n salt.
She's a resplendent butterfly...
A butterfly that cares-less if the World notices her colours.
What matters, to her, is that she:
Hovered 'n saw - glided 'n felt;
And, loved those she flew with.
She counsels all to revert to Socrates' teachings:
Nosce te ipsum - Know thyself.

14.3 You Discern the Indiscernible

The unwantin' soul;
Sees the unseeable.
The self-seekin' soul;
Sees only that it seeks.
You discern the indiscernible.
You decipher the indecipherable.
For, you're the doorway to the hidden.

>I join your continuity,
>As the shadow follows the swallows.
>Sinkin' into quietness,
>Cytherea chantry's raised.
>Self's lost;
>Humbled, I am…

>>With painless humility:
>>I celebrate you;
>>I believe in you;
>>I cherish you;
>>I adore you dear readers!

14.4 Heart that Loves

Gazin' blankly at nowhere.
I held tightly onto the last tissue-box.
A halfway expended Kleenex due to night-long waterworks.
I drowned in the rivers of my tears.
With leaden weights in the head 'n a profusely bleedin' heart;
Emotions turned unnavigable.
As untamed voice unabatedly repeated:
Push-down that heartache for a while;
Gulp those lumps of uneasiness a little longer; and,
Conceal that misery with a phony smile.
Unnatural art-of-composure I had mastered…
Unreadable book, I had become; to evade the stings of life.
But, intensity worsened with time,
Stimulatin' darkest thoughts caged within.

Like a symbol that gets no credit for being symbolic;
I surfed through the waves of life, with neither focus nor intent.
For, I was sick to the core:
Tormented by uncertainty 'n scatterbrained by nature.
As with no food I could go - my three 'Stars' couldn't.
I was an empty shell chokin' on aspirations,
Reviled by prevailin' state.
The Universe re-smiled - I smiled back.

I re-learnt to act in the livin' Present.
To leave love footprints on the sands-of-time;
Footprints, that another forlorn being, shall take heart again.
'O dear reader: Courage must come from the soul within.
You must furnish the will to win.
Crucially, be up with lips that encourage;
Palms that support 'n a heart that loves.

Chapter 15

Forgiveness

We must develop and maintain the capacity to forgive.
He who is devoid of the power to forgive is devoid of the power to love.
There is some good in the worst of us and some evil in the best of us.
When we discover this,
We are less prone to hate our enemies.

~ Martin Luther King, Jr. (1929 – 1968 AD) ~

15.1 Clear Emotions of Darkness

As you finish what you started…
In the distant horizon,
There appears a being you once knew.
Sheepishly, he pleads:
Will you help clear my path…
As I'm re-trudging down that frightful old road of life?
Can I lean on your arm for safety?

I hear you furiously protest:
Action has equal reaction!
I fearlessly proclaim:
Not e'ery action needs a preconceived action.

O' friend, break the chain of unforgiveness.
Clear your emotions of darkness.
Allow positive energy to prevail.
For, pure heart 'n soul, submit;
Truth 'n light's purity, remit;
While, forgivin' love, commit!

15.2 Forgiveness Begets Love

Forgiveness' the pure way of life.
It wipes resentfulness 'n kills indignation.
It dissolves the clamour for punishment.
For, forgiveness' the fountainhead of wellness.
Wellness for both the forgiven 'n the forgiver.
As forgiveness begets love.

Forgiveness begets love.
When we operate in forgiveness realm:
Our lives are held in solicitous hands -,
Softly in the twists 'n turns of life.
For, in forgiveness, we know:
Only a few are perfect wrongs.

Only a few are perfect wrongs – in forgiveness.
In forgiveness, we know:
Some wrongs are right.
Conversely, when we operate in revengeful sphere:
Our lives swell with anger's germs.
Germs that birth vengeful tendencies.
As anger begets anger;
While forgiveness begets true love.

15.3 Forgive and Progress

Life lessons hurt.
No exemptions from the life's school of multiple trials.
Some more than others.
Some short 'n others timeless.
A scrape on the knee,
As a memento for an innocent child.
But, must learn;
Must forgive;
And, must grow.

>Do the unplanned.
>Cherish your roses.
>Forgive those which slip through your hand.
>Anticipate all:
>Misfortune 'n bliss.
>Ever humble,
>Give the transgressor genuine kiss.

>>Be ready to forgive 'n progress.
>>As every gravelstone's unique 'n necessary.
>>Each pebble serves a role in the cascadin' creek of life;
>>Nourishin' the very gems;
>>That reveal your growth.
>>Growth through basses 'n trebles;
>>Within the symphony of forgiveness pebbles.

Chapter 16

Friendship

Friends hold a mirror up to each other.
Through that mirror they can see each other,
In ways that would not otherwise be accessible to them.
And, it is this mirroring that helps them improve themselves as persons.

~ Aristotle (384 – 322 BC) ~

16.1 Friendship Gives Value to Survival

My percipient teacher, Seneca (4 BC – 65 AD), told me:
A wise man's sufficient unto himself.
For a happy existence,
He needs only an upright soul.
But, requires help towards mere existence.
Ergo, a wise man's in want of nothing,
And yet needs many things.
He desires friends if only for the purpose of practisin' friendship.
For, friendship has no survival value;
But gives value to survival.

The majesty of friendship's the inspiration that fills us;
Once we discover the one willin' to trust us.
One ready to share our pain; and,
Caress our wounds with a tender kiss.
In his presence,
We drop our undermost garments of dissimulation;
As he faces with us the reality of our powerlessness.
He listens compassionately to our hidden silences.
For, true meaning lies concealed in the depth of the unsayable.
He thus, reflects back our own beauty through his friendship.

O' *compadre*, seek not the one who changes when you change.
Supplicate not the one who nods when you nod.
That's the role of your loyal shadow!
Instead make a friend in order to have someone,
Against whose death you may stake your own life.
For, one who seeks friendship for favourable occasions,
Strips it of its very nobility.

16.2 Friendship Makes Love Lovelier

Friendship speaks the language of the heart.
'Tis the sweetest drink.
The surest link tween Arcady 'n Earth.
Link the conceivable 'n inconceivable.
In its dew, the heart finds its morning – refreshed.

Make friends before you need them.
Trust he who sees through the sadness of your smile;
He who hears your words in your silence;
And, feels your love in your anger.
For, friendship makes love lovelier.

Trust the one who appears when all's lost 'n thorns emerged.
The one who walks on those thorns to reach you,
To bear the pain for your sake.
As there's no purpose in friendship,
Save the deepenin' of the spirit.
For, friendship that seeks aught,
Is but a net cast forth:
Only the undesirable's caught.

16.3 Friendship Makes Timid Spirit Brave

Strengthened with affection 'n care,
Friendship provides sun-warmth to the soul.
It makes timid spirit brave 'n love lovelier.
As it protects one from self-waywardness.

> A true friend embellishes your true self.
> He makes you not win to the detriment of the real winner.
> Rather, he makes you a loser,
> To edify you on how to be a polished being.
> A genuine friend shakes you from slumber;
> And, shines a light on your path.

>> Conversely, a fake friend appears in time of your equanimity,
>> And, disappears in time of despair.
>> He gives you time only when it shines,
>> But fades when it shades.
>> He's a trickster serpent – to be scorned!
>> For, better a genuine enemy than a fake friend.

16.4 True Friend Twinkles and Glows

Put friend into rhyme…
In honour of the one who's selfless beyond measure.
For, the things he does with love ne'er lack.
True friend, keeps no tabs,
But, faithfully nudges.
As he tells you the bare truth.
Hesitates not to point-out,
Whene'er your loyal third leg's cloddishly dances.
In him the commencement 'n the end harmonize.
For, his friendship surpasses flattery;
With wide-open 'n indulgent ears.
As it sinks to the depths of the heart;
And, pleases precisely wherein it harms.

True friend twinkles 'n glows - like a North Star.
He gently flows - like a deep river.
He lives without hype - like a child.
For, gentleness marks his manner;
While, honesty feeds his banner.
As, he's genuine 'n true;
With a soul full of spunk -
E'en when under gobs of pressure.

Here 'n now, I proclaim:
Uncontaminated friend's priceless.
As true friendship can be bought not;
And, genuine camaraderie can be sold not.
For, its only cost's to ensure 'tis ne'er lost.

16.5 Pleasantness of Fellowship

Each time I appraise my inner-self;
Ripples of my reflections fade.
Beyond the ripples, vision of my reflection re-emerges.
With a bond that is unbreakable;
And, synchronicity that's unmistakable;
You appear in that vision.
For, in my life, you left an eternal mark.
A mark of humanity!
Neither by choice nor the same seed.
Different mothers but souls undeniably the same breed.
Thence, let's rise by uplifting each other.
For we're respondents to Nature.

Nature impels us towards the pleasantness of fellowship.
If only for the purpose of practicing camaraderie, and
Ensurin' that our talents aren't idle.
Let's pursue a friendship clasped firmly by deep 'n true love.
Whose beauty time can't erode;
And, whose pleasure years can't erase.
Let's dream big 'n be kind to ourselves;
Let's love our uniqueness 'n express gratitude for who we're.
For, the only person we should strive to better,
Is the person we were yesterday.
And, 'tis ne'er late to be what we ought to be.

My mother – Sephora - taught me:
If you want to go quick, go alone;
If you want to go far, go together.
Faster alone further together.
Let's go together sweethearts.
Let our human frailty unite us;

Find strength in our mutual vulnerability;
Enter each other's life 'n awaken our ultimate potential.
For, unified we shall bear the stamp of divinity.
Citizens of humanity, time has come;
To rise by upliftin' one another.
To rise as one - one, and no more than one!

16.6 The Real Polaris

With the melody of footsteps,
And, the rhythm of heartbeats,
Synchronized into a calm-stillness…
I let my words fly.
Fly in the direction of an idiosyncratic being.
A gardener who consistently snips 'n clips the tangled vines.
A guide who zealously points-out the landmarks.
The landmarks to the left 'n right.
A forecaster who predicts sunshine e'en when all looks gloom.
A being whose smile calms e'en the hyena's filthy fangs,
That are ready for a feast.

O' true friend, real Polaris, you're.
For, you clear the path for others to journey.
You bring what's beyond the eyes into reality.
You lighten heavy thoughts;
Liven numb feelings;
Quieten unsteady hearts;
And, dry drippin' tears;
Revealin' the essence of life.
As you're ingenious 'n fair.
Humane 'n loveable.

O' *amigo*, keep shinnin' 'n bein' an inspiration to humanity;
Be the reason someone believes in the goodness in humankind.
Keep the light within you greater than the darkness around,
And, continue being a star!
In mind to keep though:
Stars do not pull each other down to be more visible;
They shine brighter.
Smile brighter *rafiki*!

16.7 Gardener who makes Souls Blossom

Throughout the year,
Snowflakes ooze from your office's walls.
Some stellar-shaped, others fern-like.
All purest of the pure.
As your office's a workshop of love.
A workshop that brings love to the lonely,
And, hope to the lost.

Dear charming grdener, you're like a bow,
From which others' as livin' arrows are sent-forth.
You remain faithful with a singleness of aim:
Stoopin' ne'er for worldly state.
Your high endeavours are an inward light,
That makes the path for others e'er bright.
Brings them alive to tenderness; and,
Shields them from the distress of dark-imaginings.
In spite of the noisy confusion of life,
You enable all keep peace with their souls.
You remind them:
The harder you're thrown, the higher you bounce.
As, the Universe unfolds in perfection.

O' *amicus*, your presence generates,
A feelin' of excitement 'n peace.
A feelin' of the beauty 'n the spirit of humanity.
A spirit sustained by your heart-warmin' smile.
For you spread cheer 'n reflect light,
With your altruistic impulses.
Impulses of a charmin' gardener who makes souls blossom.
You're a testimony that e'en in the face of disenchantment;
Love's perpetual.

16.8 Friend: The Music in the Song

Here comes one 'n the only one…
The one whose office's a place of no walls.
An office with a picture of thousand colors 'n thousand sounds.
A picture polished by fresh winds –
Tacked onto the air.
A beautiful scenery e'en when stormy.
Had the honor to taste her hands.
Hands e'er ready to straighten a wayward bow.
Hands e'er there to caress a hurt;
And, to hold stars in place.
Had the honor to taste her tongue.
A tongue that exudes hope 'n happiness.
A tongue that oozes sagesse 'n thoughtfulness.
O' yeah, time with her is unmovin'…, untellin'…
For, like the Sun warmin' a seagull -
Each moment has its own chapter.

> 'O dear friend,
> You're the rose in the vase.
> You're the music in the song.
> The serene song of the Universe,
> That stirs waters with timeless opal.
> You're the shine on a dark gloomy day…
> You still the talk.
> You make brightness where'er you walk.
> As, you're strong in e'ery way.
> Untiringly, you remind all:
> We're beautiful when we wear our lights.
> For, love's light…

My mother, Sephora, edified me:
Choose carefully who you stand beside -
For, with certain shadows, shadows hide.
I stand beside you *mon ami(e)*.
As, like sunlight upon scintillatin' waters –
You lights up…
Fallin' 'n callin' to the purity of heavens.

16.9 Your Time to Soar

Life is a series of *karibu na kwaheri;*
Bonjour et au revoir;
Hellos and goodbyes.
In preparation for things bigger 'n better.
For, the goddess of the art of soaring has proclaimed:
Time to soar!

Friend, workin' with you was a journey of growth.
For, you didn't only bid me into your deep well of wisdom;
But, you led me to the threshold of my soul.
You are smart, engagin' yet unpretentious.
For, you think with your heart.
I savoured your clean thinkin'.
Thinkin' marked by focus 'n clarity - finesse 'n elegance.
E'er with a genuine smile 'n a givin' heart.
As you're filled with an infectious positivity…
Positivity that's hard not to share.
But now, the horns are soundin'.
As, the verdict's out: Your time to soar's here!

'O dear, the road's ready for you.
For, the wind's at your backs.
Let the sky be your limit.
Ride towards high to better see the world;
And, not for the world to see you.
Thence, believe 'n support those you work with;
Appreciate 'n motivate 'em - empower 'n uplift 'em.
Soar with 'em dear friends.
For, that's the pinnacle of the art of soaring!

Chapter 17

Happiness

True happiness is to enjoy the present,
Without anxious dependence upon the future.
Not to amuse ourselves with either hopes or fears,
But to rest satisfied with what we have,
Which is sufficient,
For he that is so,
Wants nothing.

~ Seneca the Younger (4 BC – 65 AD) ~

17.1 Let Joy be You

Follow the lights of awakenin'.
And rejoice in pure humanity;
Become light, free 'n shinin'.
But easier 'tis to see another's fault,
While ours, we hide.
Be forewarned: Dwellin' on another's fault,
Multiplies our own.
It distracts us from the journey.
For, the way isn't in the sky,
But in our hearts.

Throughout the journey of life:
Mirror what you admire;
Reflect what you desire;
Attract what you expect;
Become what you respect.
Like uncovered candle, chase away darkness.
Let your star shine 'n reveal your soul.
Within, without, keep shinin'.
Break-free 'n rise in the illimitable air.
Let hope 'n joy be where'er you reside,
In the country 'n in the city - generate hope.
In the valley 'n in the hills - generate joy.

'Drink' deeply;
Live in serenity 'n felicity.
And, let the gods of goodliness admire you.
Remember though: what we do to 'n for others outlast us.
For, they're like pyramids in pharaohs' honour.
Only made out of the memories others have of us.

17.2 Happiness is Never Perfected Until it is Shared

Show me a mortal who wishes to be tickled;
Day 'n night with an orgasmatron.
And, I'll show you a mind-soul devoid of contentment.
For, a harmonized body-mind-soul is the gateway to happiness.
And, singleness of being begets eudæmonia.
Like empyrean light,
Jollity reflects the shinin' rays of munificence.
As 'tis the sunbeam that passes through bosoms,
Without losin' a particle of its original ray.
For, it diminishes not for being shared.

Seek not happiness at the peak of the mountain of life,
Cultivate it under your feet, as you climb.
For 'tis the climbin' that matters.
Its secret's no secret.
As there's no path to happiness - happiness' the path.
A path you can journey not, 'til you become the path itself;
'Til you attain Sun's magnificence.
So magnificent: one can't e'en look at her.

Grow beauty in your eyes.
Inflate your lungs with an onrush of scenery:
Mountains, valleys, trees, air, rivers, sea…
And, be the charmin' gardener who makes souls blossom.
For, happiness is only real when shared,
And, diminishes not for being shared.
On your own, you must stand;
If you're to revel real happiness.
Go to the left where nothing's right 'n see light;
Swing to the right where nothing's left 'n be light.
Jump onto the ripest chord of the void song 'n find truth.

Throw self into the wilderness, and find her…
For within you, she rests, waitin' to be aroused.
Think well of self 'n proclaim it to the world.
Not through uproarious words but unexcelled deeds.
For, happiness' ne'er perfected 'til 'tis shared.

17.3 Gateway to Being Young at Heart

Assemble your ladder to the stars.
Climb on e'ery rung.
Be righteous 'n see the lights surroundin' self.
For, that's the gateway to being young at heart.
When the winds of change blow.
Stand upright 'n steady.
Nourish your brain 'n dance your dance.
Be joyous!
For, that's the gateway to being young at heart.

> We're what we think.
> As we arise with our thoughts.
> Act with a pure mind 'n youngness will follow you.
> Like the wheels follow the ox that draws the cart.
> That's the law, ancient and inexhaustible.

>> Fabricate your happiness.
>> Revel in good food;
>> Cherish sound sleep;
>> Relish solid rhythmic sex 'n relax.
>> Inject happiness into your heart;
>> And, you'll be un-uprootable.
>> For, wind can't overturn a mountain.
>> And, temptation can't touch a (wo)man,
>> Who masters self.
>> For, one who masters self, is a happy (wo)man.
>> He sees the false as false 'n true as true.
>> For, he follows authentic Nature.
>> For, that's the gate-way to being young at heart.

Chapter 18

Goodliness

*It is easy to perform a good action,
But not easy to acquire a settled habit of performing such actions.*

~ Aristotle (384-322 BC) ~

*How far that little candle throws its beams!
So shines a good deed in a naughty world.*

~ William Shakespeare (1564-1616 AD) ~

18.1 Real Goodness Emanates from Within

Pressed a $20 bill into my ten-years old son's steady hands;
For his favourite meal in an ice-hockey game…
Approachin' a dishevelled old man on the frigid sidewalk:
The boy unhesitatingly pressed the $20 bill,
Into the man's tremblin' hands.
An authentic warm lockin' of eyes in acknowledgment ensued.
He edified me: altruism's not mere givin'.
'Tis being present through the wavy vision:
Vision of the self's heat – love on firm averment.
And, real goodness emanates from a deeper reservoir within.

Ne'er give to receive.
For, there's more joy in givin' than in receivin'.
Awaken to the righteousness of doin' that's virtuous;
For you see the intrinsic nobility.
Not to be cited in a preposterous roll of honour;
And, massage a bloated runaway ego.
Tread lightly 'n dive-in with a weeny splash;
And, beseech the cosmos to sing your song.
That's the sifted altruistic axiomatic asseveration to Gæa.

Dwell not in an egoic self-designed fellowless firmament;
But, in an abode by the highway of life,
Where the race of the half-good 'n the half-bad goes-by.
Venture beyond the waves off your fire.
Rejoice when passersby rejoice; and,
Weep with their moans.
For, in tryin' to soothe another's woes,
Yours evanesce.
And, you can ne'er be what you ought to be;
'Til they're what they ought to be.

18.2 Became a Drop

Today, I awoke to a garden of golden flowers,
A bouquet of words that blooms from within-without.
I woke to a dream of a quest that yearns to begin.
As warm sunlight opens petals,
I encountered enchanted words that enlighten.
Words that brighten the soul –
Birthin' a garden of brilliance - in e'ery hue.

But, with fear,
The mighty river trembles;
Before enterin' the Ocean.
In her face, she sees an Ocean.
An Ocean so vast that to enter,
Is to lose her identity - to disappear.
But, she can go back not.
For, goin' back is unnatural in the journey of life.
Thenceso, the mighty river takes the risk,
And, dive deep into the Ocean…
Alas! She realizes she disappeared not.
Rather, she became the Ocean.
I-became-a-drop-of-humanity!

As a drop, humanity edified me to venture within -
Venturin' without is deep.
Humanity illuminated my inner oracle decks -
The straight route to higher self.
Humanity taught me how to play to the rattle of my raw forks -
I feel the thrill of glory from head to toe.
As I-became-a-drop-of-Humanity: the Ocean!

As a drop, I do what drops ought to do - challenge all:

Build the new – fight not the tired.
Let your soul show 'n make darkness conscious.
Instil a different genre of immunity in humanity.
Walk far 'n much.
Into the river – walk 'n cross;
Into the Ocean – walk 'n cross.
The extent to which you can walk in the other's shoes.
…Be as enthusiastic about the success of the 'other' as you're about yours…
…Have no time to hate…
Let the hills echo your good.
And, instil immunity in humanity.

18.3 Take Time to Know

Take time to know the 'Other'…
And you will see,
He isn't the Monster you heard/read/dreamt of.
Give him a chance…
And you will realize,
Although imperfect,
He has a heart that beats 'n blood that reds.

> Take time to know the 'Other'…
> Just give it a try,
> And, you'll see that you are'nt that different - you 'n him.
> He errs – don't you?
> Take time to know him…
> What have you got to lose,
> Besides the ignorance you feed on?
> Choose not twix him 'n ignorance.
> For, you know your choice.

>> In the name of goodliness,
>> Take time to know the 'Other' –
>> 'Tis all what's necessary…
>> No great feat
>> Just play in waves that kiss the shore;
>> And, know him.
>> Enjoy the twilight hours more;
>> As you know him.
>> Wish upon the twinlkin' stars,
>> For, only now is yours 'n him – goodliness.

18.4 Real Goodness Emanates from Within

O' goodliness:
In the vastness of space 'n the immensity of time,
My eyes have met your golden silhouettes…
My touch has met your cascadin' curves…
My soul drums to the beat of your unclouded heart…

O' goodliness:
I dream with the taste of you in my taste-buds.
For, you're more than fruit 'n blossom.
You're more than the sum of your parts.

O' goodliness:
You're worth all my fight.
(T)hencefore, I hold self supremely blest.
So, I let the children of Zeus flourish…
…Through you!

Chapter 19

Femininity

A woman is a lyre.
She only reveals her secrets to those who know how to play.

~ Honoré de Balzac (1799-1850 AD) ~

19.1 Loyal to the Love of Love

I choose to follow where the path leads not.
To hills untopped 'n valleys unexplored.
Fared too far to turn back, I have.
To sell my soul for a song.
So, I explore the dreams she dreams 'n the spirit of beauty.
Beauty, whose sweet impulses,
Flushes the exalted consciousness,
With shafts of sensible divinity.

A mirror, reflects, unconditionally.
A woman, provides 'n protects.
E'er a refuge, ne'er a refugee.
She quivers with cosmic passion;
And, walks in fellowship with winds 'n clouds.
For, she's joy diffused in purest communion.
That bears the image of the deity's masterplan.
Through her womb, that swells for birth,
Divine strength's revealed.
Reflectin' Maker's heart;
Pregnant with creation's worth.

Through her, signs are laid bare in wholesome light.
Praisin' glory at the sight: She's woman - the temple.
The elegance of her shape!
Endowed with a smooth 'n steadfast mind;
Gentle thoughts 'n calm desires.
Like perfume in the laden flower,
Interfused throughout the whole:
She's the humanity's pulse 'n soul.
For, she's loyal to the love of love.

19.2 Woman: Portal Between Spiritual and Physical Realms

Woman's beauty innate.
Life-giver;
Miracle-creator; and,
Magic-maker, she's.
Born with the wisdom of sibyls,
She blooms e'en in the dead of night.
For, she's the thread of life.

Womanhood's the sacred water.
The sacred water that quenches the Universe's thirst:
Through her elegant eyes 'n enchantin' soul;
Splendour of acts 'n gracefulness of being.
She's the epithet of simplicity 'n finesse:
The Ace!

O' sister, like the mythical Phoenix,
Certain of your worth, soar-free.
Express your desires 'n live your dreams.
Dance your dance like you've got zircons,
At the meeting of your thighs…
Well 'n swell, and bring the virtuous gifts past infinity.
As you're nature's wings 'n tide of life:
While the hill might feel steep and the climb slow –
The climbin' is the key.

19.3 Feminine Beauty

Feminine beauty twinkles with abandon.
For, a woman's a *chef-d'œuvre* of creation.
She's lovely in her bones.
When she sighs, birds sigh back.
When she moves, she moves in multiple ways.
For, her beauty grows 'n glows with time.
Unforgivingly 'n forcefully magnificent...

> Woman's beauty radiates from her eyes;
> The pathway to her soul.
> From the soul,
> Her allure weaves in e'ery raven ringlet.
> Lightenin' o'er her face;
> Serenely 'n eloquently.

>> O' sister!
>> Say to self: I am beautiful.
>> Say to self: I am unparalleled.
>> Say to 'em: You appreciate not my elegance;
>> You deserve my attention not.
>> For, you're the wellspring of humanity.
>> As, Deity writes in stars through feminity.

19.4 Deep-sea of Feminity

Diversity within the deep-sea feminine heart,
Is the determination that unifies humanity.
And, e'ery girl's that unflinchin' resoluteness.
Thence, give her tools to venture into the uncharted path.
Feminity's beauty innate.

Diversity within the deep-sea feminine heart,
Reveals the beauty of Universe.
A woman with a voice can move worlds.
She can make the broken beautiful 'n the strong invincible.
Feminity's beauty innate.

Diversity within the deep-sea feminine heart,
Makes us strong.
Respect her 'n keep her near.
Love her 'n keep her dear.
For, a society's as strong as the health of its womenfolk.
Feminity's beauty innate.

Chapter 20

Parenthood

*Once you have your children;
You understand what you owe your parents.*

~ Japanese Proverb ~

20.1 We are Strong and Ready to Soar

O' father - O' mother!
Who do I talk with?
For, Facebook's your breakfast 'n Instagram's your lunch;
WhatsApp's your afternoon snack 'n Twitter's your dinner.
In-tween, headphones are your oxygen;
While your touchscreen-tablet zigs 'til the break of dawn.
Please calm your hands 'n mind - and, talk to me.
Engage your ears 'n heart - and, listen to me.

O' mother: When will you re-tell the tale of *the Beauty 'n the Beast*?
When Facebook-Instagram goes off?
O' father: When will you play hide 'n seek with me?
When your Twitter-WhatsApp dies?
Please talk to me with your hands 'n mind free;
Talk to me with your ears 'n heart engaged.
For, you're the reason I awakened.

Parents of the world:
You're the meanin' of our existence - our wave centre.
But, the golden wave's takin' unknown direction:
Crashin' at the shores.
Clack, click, clink, snick - lives are stolen in a flash...
Facebook, Instagram, Twitter 'n WhatsApp are the robbers.
They've turned our lives upside-down inside-out.
Turned frowns into smiles;
And, smiles into frowns.
They breathe turmoil into our young souls,
Makin' us cry when we want to laugh;
And, laugh when we want to cry.
As you blankly stare at us as if we weren't there...
But, we're here – ready for a take-off.

20.2 Bequeath to Your Children the Spirit of Reverence

In the silent sacrament of life;
Fatherhood goes unsung 'n unpraised.
As father's dreams 'n worries are seldom spoken.
But, what goes silent in a father speaks in the son;
And, in the daughter, is the unveiled secret of a father.
In his presence, glamorous furrows engrave in the heart,
As he conveys in his lovin' touch the fine art,
And gentle shapin' of life.
Thence, he merits lovin' compliments 'n accolades of praise.
For, he gives his younglings something mythical,
And, infinitely apposite.

Fatherhood's a noble endeavour.
For, the impression made by a fatherly voice,
Sets a lovely trend of life.
Sets a solid foundation through the storms of life.
From the pits of his id 'n his malleable superego,
He provides tools to escape the dung of baser nature.
Thus, like a magician who fishes rabbits out of his hat,
He draws love from his raw heart;
While the rivers of his hands overflow with aureate deeds.

The past teaches the present - so does a father to his young-ones.
A daughter needs a father to show her,
How to find steel in her heart;
A son needs a father to edify him how to read the life map.
Thence, tell your youngsters not how to live;
Rather, live 'n let them taste you in action.
For, one day they'll live your model.
So, bequeath to your children the spirit of reverence.

20.3 Profession of Auntiship

Let's sing the song.
My Auntie's song.
Words fly-up and away;
As they form.
But, I've to sing my auntie's song.

> O' how beautiful she is...
> Her hair, pretty - her smile, witty;
> Her voice, sweet - her eyes, lovely.
> For, my auntie's heart's made of golden love.
> Elegancy 'n purity define her.
> Strength 'n wisdom define her being.
> Generosity 'n care define her e'ery contour.
> While creativity's her code-name.
> As, only her sewing machine comprehends her artistic-tongue.

>> O' Auntie, cherished friend – you remain.
>> Personal cheerleader;
>> Who saw me through muddled pedagogical lenses.
>> You contributed to the formation of my philosophical soul.
>> You taught me:
>> If you know not to which port you're sailin';
>> No wind' favourable.
>> I think of you with pride.
>> I cherish you with endearment.
>> For, through you the profession of auntiship's a fine art.

20.4 Motherhood: Hallowed Service to Humanity

Mother!
A term that embodies love in its purest form:
Unconditional 'n boundless;
Unflaggin' 'n flawless -
Total...
Human heart isn't meant to beat outside the body;
Yet, a child represents a mother's heart.
A heart beatin' outside her rib-cage.
For, in her child she finds a piece of herself apart:
Smells the scent of her own skin;
And, feels the map of her own skeleton-sled.

Motherhood's a Sisyphean task:
No sooner a seam's sewn-shut, anew rips-open.
Motherhood's influence is ungainsayable:
Exchange of nothing for the possibility of everything.
Motherhood's power defies natural laws:
Creatin' something out of nothing.

Motherhood's luminescence,
That connects humankind to divinity:
The hallowed service to humanity.
O' mothers, to you, I bow in reverence!
For, you're the chalice that births life.
The wellhead that nourishes growth; and,
The sea of flames that spreads love 'n hope.
By raisin' children who make the world less heartless.

20.5 Motherhood: Where Love Begins and Ends

Mother's heart wanders with her children.
For, motherhood's where love begins 'n ends.
The greatest love of 'em all.
Love that deciphers the unsaid.

Motherhood's where love begins 'n thrives.
As mothers are:
A gingerbread that eases fears;
And, a kiss that kills tears.

Motherhood's where love thrives 'n ends.
As mothers are:
A smile that guides the way;
A comfort that lightens the night.
A sunshine that lights the day.

Chapter 21

Beauty

*We should infer in the case of a beautiful dwelling-place,
That it was built for its owners and not for mice.
We ought, therefore, in the same manner,
To regard the Universe as the dwelling-place of the gods.*

~ Chrysippus (279 – 206 BC) ~

21.1 Beauty's Life

Beautiful the smallest deed any day
Than the wondrous wrapped gift that was never given;
Or, the greatest intention tucked away.

Beautiful is the trial of life.
For, there's beauty in struggle,
As, there's feelin' in pain.

Beautiful is the learnin'.
For, in every painstakin' mistake in life,
There are lessons to be named.
Beauty's life.

21.2 Beauty Renders Irrational Rational

In the immensity of time;
And, the vastness of space:
When figures show their royal front;
And, sense from spirit fades…
When that which was,
That which is,
And, that which will, fusion…
I elect one.

I select one whose beauty teaches love.
For, she's like the Sun that bows to kiss Moon's feet.
She's the colours of the commonest;
And, scarce of diadems.
Life's a different wealth - with her:
She's a veritable gem.
A gem that renders nonsensible sensible;
Illogical logical; and,
Irrational rational.

'O gem:
From heaven below to heaven above;
I feel your presence in your absence.
For, two hearts danced to the immortal tune,
'Til clocks ticked softly 'n rhythmically into one.
Like a distant moon your beauty leads my sea,
Along appointed sands…
With your amber hands of beauty.

21.3 Epicentre of Beauty

Done with the compass - free-rowin' in Eden!
Chance can't dent my want for your beauty;
Nor time impair.
For, thy singleness of soul makes me proud.
Proud of your innate beauty.

    Thy purity of heart makes me love aloud.
    Think it - feel it;
    Obdurate no more.
    Just pick 'n light your lamp,
    And, march – this beautiful match...

        You're beautiful when adornin' your light.
        Breathe it into being;
        And, coax it onto eternal nothingness.
        Coax it with pure love;
        And, rejoice with equal passion 'n joy.
        And, that's the epicentre of beauty.

Chapter 22

Character

Well, I am certainly wiser than this man.
It is only too likely that neither of us has any knowledge to boast of;
But he thinks that he knows something which he does not know,
Whereas I am quite conscious of my ignorance.
At any rate it seems that I am wiser than he is to this small extent,
That I do not think that I know what I do not know.

~ Socrates (470 – 399 BC) ~

22.1 Trust Self when all Doubt You

My esteemed Sensei, Morihei Ueshiba (1883 - 1969), told me:
Iron's full of impurities that weaken it.
Through fire, steel, then transformed into a razor-sharp sword.
Beings develop in the same fashion.
For, life is a cycle - at times painful!
But, that's what forges your character.
Body-mind-soul refinement shapes your destiny!

Quirkiness...
Haecceity...
Helps you find your natural balance.
Strive for excellence not perfection.
For, you can always be better than you were.
Trust self when all doubt you.
Wait when tired of waitin',
Give way not to hatin' when hated.
Dedicate to what gives your life meanin';
And, make a positive difference to those you interact with.

Dream but not make your dream your master;
Think but not make your thoughts your aim;
Talk with crowds but not lose your virtue;
Dine with non-commoners but not lose your common touch.
Perceive that cannot be seen;
By seein' with your ears 'n hearin' with your eyes.
For, that's the mastery of full-livin'.
Within-without, keep your star shinin'.

22.2 Be Bold in Pursuit of Self

To quit inner character to assume the external,
Is to be ignorant.
Those who quit are ignorant,
Both of the character they leave 'n of the character they assume.
For, they tell themselves lies about selves.
They fear being different 'n lack character.

Character forges in the full current of life.
Never develops in ease 'n quiet.
For, only through trial is the soul strengthened.
And, the ultimate measure's where one stands at times of adversity.
With a refined character the eye rejoices 'n body's warmed.
With polished character the heart expands 'n the soul's cheered.

So, be bold in your avid pursuit of self.
And, whenever you see one of a contrary character,
Turn inwards and examine self – deep.
Be a fool every so often…
Learn something out of every folly…
Repeat none though –
But, arrive at intimate understandin'.
As there can be no failure to a man,
Who hasn't lost his character.

22.3 Be Character

Character preaches a finer sermon.
So, be naturally simple 'n decent,
Have lazy days seekin' your deep.

    Character preaches a better sermon.
    So, wear your gentle heart 'n quiet mind;
    And, restrain your temper 'n tongue.

        Character preaches a superior sermon than lips.
        So, let patience triumph over pride.
        With charity for those who err –
        Be as you wish to seem.
        Be Character.

22.4 Know a Thing

Worship whoever you adore.
But, know a thing:
Tributes paid in the dark recesses of our hearts,
Will out.

Worship whatever you want.
But, know a thing:
A man should not wish to enjoy,
Where he does not give joy.

Worship howsoever you wish.
But, know a thing:
That which dominates your thoughts determine your character.
For, what you're thinkin' you're becomin'.

22.5 Be a Teacher

Be a lighthouse.
Be a motivator.
Be a teacher.
A teacher's a lighthouse.
A lighthouse that guides.
Guides ships through the turbulent darkness.

Be a lighthouse.
Be a motivator.
Be a teacher.
A teacher lights the path.
Lights the right path for students.
Motivates them to dream 'n reach.
To know, to grow 'n to glow.

Be a lighthouse.
Be a motivator.
Be a teacher.
A teacher molds students into precious gems.
By helpin' them walk upon the unwalked.
For, he sees potential 'n believes in the best in others.
He births a seed of curiosity 'n endearment.

Chapter 23

Well Wishes

*Be the bird.
The bird perched on a frail branch,
That she feels bending beneath her.
Still she sings away all the same,
Knowing she has capable wings.*

~ Victor Hugo (1802 – 1885 AD) ~

23.1 Complete Someone's Song

May your well overflow…
As your well of beingness overflows,
Open the garden of your kind thoughts.
Open your garden 'n discover beauty beneath the scars.

As your well of beingness overflows,
Embolden your cares with:
Eyes that see the invisible; and,
Ears that hear the unsayable.
Enliven your cares with:
A heart that beats with empathy; and,
A soul that bears what the 'other' bears.

As your well of beingness overflows,
Forget not - e'ery heart sings a song.
An incomplete song,
'Til another heart whispers back.
So, complete someone's song –
Be his hero.
My hero - you're!

Have a joyous Year-end;
Et, bonne anneé 2018!

23.2 May You be the Way I See You

The old gives way to the new.
As the old skin must be shed-off,
For the transcendin' beauty to emerge.
Thence, the magical bell of translucent ice's singin'.
Announcin' the new-beginning 'n another-beginning's end.
Usherin' in a fugacious time:
When stillness suspends vitality;
And, passions grapple with callithump of fashions.
Callin' us to make the world a better place for all.

O' reader let the world know your gentleness.
Calm her anger 'n slow her rush - through livin' from your heart.
Let not hate dictate your thoughts, words 'n deeds -
By openin'-up your soul.
For, it feels better to hold hands;
And, to make the world a warmer place for the other.

In this new-beginnin', go-forth with a purpose true,
And, uplift the unknown along the journey of life.
For, there's more joy in givin' than in recievin'.
Absorb the stones 'n let them sink into your waters.
For, their accumulation brings the surface to new heights;
Formin' ornate beauties.
An authentic reflection of heavenly glories; and,
A livin' nourishment to humanity.
May you be the way I see you:
Genuine, carin' 'n loveable.

Wish you a year to behold.
Bonne année 2019!

23.3 Share the Glow of Your Smile

The tree's pregnant with potential wonder.
Jingle-bells are on.
Coloured lights are on 'n off;
With their flames of joy brightenin' the globe.
Timeless carols of sweet melodies repeat:
Good-will-to-all!
Marked by graceful rhythms of the sky.
Like swallows singin' down each blowin' wind.
Makin' the Yuletide scenery's lovelier than landscapes in a dream.
For, this is the time!

>This is the time to consider the needs of the 'other'.
>To help the 'other' brave the thickenin' ills of life.
>The time to share the glory of a cheerful smile.
>For, it takes a spark of a genuine smile,
>To lighten the heavy cloud the 'other' bears.

>>A genuine smile is like a candle's glow.
>>A glow whose fullness remains intact;
>>No matter the number of candles it glows.
>>With a gentle touch thence,
>>Share the glow of your smile.
>>For, this' the time!

>>>*Happy festive period;*
>>>*And, 2020 full of success.*

23.4 Life's Fresh Every Nouvel Dawn

A wave's driven by a wave.
Each pursued pursues the wave ahead.
Likewise, time flies on 'n follows - flies 'n follows.
What was before is left behind;
What ne'er was is now.
E'ery passin' moment's renewed.
As the old yields to the new;
And, 2019 melts into 2020.

Life's fresh e'ery novel dawn:
It signals rejuvenescence.
So, as the mortal mist gathers;
Breathe in the Heaven's applause – in confidence.
For the planets that square your moon matter less.
Let the ecstasy of wildness fill to your nosetip;
And, risk lookin' fatuous for your adventure(s) of being alive.
Be free from your fear.
For, as we get liberated from our fear,
Our presence liberates others.

As 2019 matures to 2020.
Be virtuous with fellow travellers of life.
Speak your truth quietly, clearly 'n frankly;
And, take kindly the counsel of the years.
Bear the accusation of betrayal without betrayin' your soul.
Be lost without being a loser;
Be fractured without being broken;
And, fail without being a failure...
Be a willow that bends without breakin'.
Function thence, at a pace that pulls you apart not.
Beyond a wholesome discipline though:

Honour things that make you alive.

Be gentle with self.
Be cheerful in 2020.

23.5 True Happiness is in Making Others Happy

The gale has fettered the gurglin' rill.
Maple trees are bare 'n blue-jays are aphonic.
But, coloured lights are twinklin',
While bells are chimin' the old special melodious sound:
Peace on earth 'n goodwill to all…
With eyes sparkled with merriment,
Children are dancin' to the nature's beauteous poetry.

Children are dancin' to announce fresh promise of Yuletide.
In the spirit of givin' thence,
Swim across the sea of life 'n startle the aquatics.
Sprinkle your multifarious weightlessness 'n ring out the false.
Submit to the rhapsodies of your heart 'n ring in the true.
Divorce indifference 'n suppress bitterness.
For, with love, storms are no storms;
Debris are whole 'n ruins picture unity.
So, radiate light of endearment; sound the trumpet of rebirth;
And, bring jollity to hearts of all.

Children are merrily dancin' to mark the end of 2020.
But, in the choreographed dance of life, endings birth beginnings.
For, end of a melody isn't its goal,
But, a melody reaches not its goal without the end.
And, sunset's the backside of sunrise.
So, rise 'n strike your harp 'n let it ring.
Suck the snakebite of hate; and,
Instil the ability to understand 'n cope.
Teach dark holes how to shine 'n spread honour 'n hope.
Weave your multi-coloured love onto plain nests; and,
Magnify lives with kindliness 'n thoughtfulness.
Give every livin' creature a smile 'n let the holly be holy.

For, true happiness' (in) makin' others happy.

May the peace of Yuletide guard your mind 'n soul.
May the glad dawn of 2021 shower your body 'n heart with solid health.

23.6 Let Your Dreams Find Truth in what You Pursue

Trees are twinklin' 'n carols are singin'.
Jingle-bells are soundin' 'n fresh-cut pines are lit…
…Wreaths are upon the doors.
For, the special time of the year's upon us:
The time to give 'n to serve.
The time to share 'n to spread good cheer.
To put love 'n kindness in action.
In the spirit of Yuletide.

> Open your eyes 'n hear the impeccable rhythm.
> Open your ears 'n see the incredible view.
> Unwrap the stupendous gift nature offers you incessantly.
> For, each day has a glorious start.
> Marked by sounds of crystal tones 'n vibrant harmony.
> That set your body-soul-spirit into a perfect synchronization.
> Which feed the golden thread that enjoins humanity.
> In harmony with the very spirit of good-tide.

> O' dear reader, uplift the other.
> Create a comfortin' sensation; and,
> Generate a radiance of hope.
> Throughout laugh, love 'n enjoy the fun.
> Let your dreams find truth in what you
> Pursue 'n let peace dwell in you, richly.

> *Have a joyous year-end;*
> *Et, bonne Année 2021!*

23.7 Align Your Lamp

Snow on snow.
Frosty wind moans.
As Cherubim 'n Seraphim throng the air.
For the time has come – again.
A time when cheer 'n gladness blend.
When heart meets heart,
And good meets good.
A time to align our lamps.

Align your lamp to give more light.
For, life's long for love to live.
Life's short for bitterness to cease.
Stoop down 'n consider the needs of the needy.
Stop 'n remember the loneliness of the lonely.
Unravel your tangles 'n smoothen your rough edges.
Carry your lamp in front 'n let your shadow fall behind you.
Align your lamp to give less smoke.

Align your lamp to give more light 'n less smoke.
Let glorious-light light your soul.
Open the gates of your garden of kindliness,
And, let peace hearten your heart.
As the old gives way to the fresh,
Align your lamp 'n open your gates.
As the old gives way to the new,
May serenity 'n joy thrill your day;
May love 'n peace fill your way;
May health 'n hope seal your sway.

May your year have a treasurable end.
May your year have a memorable start.

PART TWO

YANG OF LIFE

Chapter 24

Egotism

Egotism is a false self,
Created by unconscious identification with one's mind.
It tricks you to think that you are ascending,
When in reality you are descending at a dizzying speed.

~ Kibicho (2019: page 117) ~

24.1 Vulture on a Human Spirit

Egoic sprites exhale mythopoeism.
They generate vultures on human spirit.
Toxic vultures that draw their fine essence from the fadin' brain:

Egoic sprites create blind spots in the mind.
Spots that read like cheat-preacher's idiocies:
My bowels deliver rare earths 'n I sail west to reach east…

Egoic sprites beget illusion.
Beget an illusory man who reasons thus:
So divine so ethereal, I am…
I can't be comprehended, except by my permission.
A tragedy of the one so 'hip' e'en his missteps are saintly!

24.2 Egoic Man

An egoic man's egoic.
So hip, his inflated ego takes him to a treacherous path.
A path through deep woods where neither path nor woods exist.

An egoic man's flatulent.
For, like flatulent distension in helium balloon,
He floats around: bloated 'n empty.
Swellin' out unmanageably.
Enthralled by unconquerable delusion,
His iridescent persona swims through self-orgiastic pool of life.

An egoic man's membranes are clogged.
For, his inner membranes are clogged with self-deceptions,
Slowin' down his life's eminent clock.
As, a ship for nocuous parasites, he is.

24.3 Deflate Your Swollen Ego

O' you of swollen ego.
You of fake ambience of self-importance.
I say: through genuine filters of ego,
We give meanin' to that we hear, touch, taste, see 'n feel.

    O' you of untamed ego.
    You of self-serving illusory fairy tales.
    I note: with tamed ego,
    We birth an aura of ordered unselfishness.
    Shiftin' the epicentre of our beingness,
    Beyond the borders of our phenomenal self.

        O' you of bloated ego.
        Deflate your swollen ego,
        And, reveal your transcendent significance in life.
        As we live in ourselves 'n in others.
        So, shine your soul with the moon's egoless humility,
        And, endearments will attend you abundantly.

Chapter 25

Poor Leadership

Characteristics of a poor leader:
A horrible voice, bad breeding and a vulgar manner.
For, a demagogue must neither be educated nor honest;
He has to be both ignoramus and rogue.

~ Aristophanes (444 – 385 BC) ~

25.1 The Fart that Pollutes

The night was clearer than the day.
As the fart of the day still pollutes.
As they crossbred mosquitoes with armadillos.
As they crossbred salamanders with vipers.
Givin' birth to callous moronic ogres.
Ogres that differentiate not tween left 'n right.
Turnin' humanity into a cacophony of anarchy.
Cacophony of anarchy.
Anarchy.

The fart of the day still pollutes.
As they crossbred mosquitoes with vipers.
Givin' birth to callous moronic ogres.
Ogres that form morbid circles.
Circles that no goodwill could penetrate.
A circle that deploys its carcinogenic sting wide 'n far,
Makin' commoners believe they're the polluters.
While televising propaganda of the good it stands for.
But, what it stands for,
Stands on sad sand.
Sad.

The fart of the day still pollutes.
As they crossbred armadillos with salamanders.
Givin' birth to callous moronic ogres.
Ogres that spoon-fed the plebeians with pseudo-freedom.
Puttin' humanity in shackles 'n hackles.
Curse be all who sheathed their swords;
For, what goes around;
Comes around 'n burns.
Burns.

25.2 Sycophancy's Bled by Leeches

From the thraldom of the ages,
'Tis as certain as the settin' of the Sun;
Sycophancy's bled by leeches,
And, dished-out by villainous fake-leaders.
'Tis fertilized by misery 'n watered with tears.
As we injudiciously turn our world into a sycophant society.
As we bring selves in full communion with:
True pomp 'n chivalry;
Killer bows 'n arrows; and,
Spineless rascals 'n senseless sycophants –
Rapists of truthful genes...
With which psychotic joy-suckers [fake leaders] are surrounded.

At fullness of sycophant malady,
The masses whisper to selves:
Let's praise him - he's our man.
Let's impress him - we need to use this chance.
Free-flyin' invitation cards to nowhere announce:
'Tis-our-time-to-eat.
For, we no longer kiss a spade a spade!

Look for no Moses to lead you out of this sycophantic wilderness.
For, if you get one 'n he gets you to the promised-land;
A blood-suckin' Judas will drain the swamp 'n lead you out.
Stand erect in the majesty of your humanness.
Listen to the authentic throbbin' of your inner voice,
And you'll discern the quickstep marches –
To Camp-Mental-Freedom.

25.3 Listen to the Throbbing of Your Inner voice

Sigmund Freud (1856 - 1939) subtly reminds me:
If the powerful executes oppression well…
If the oppressor oppresses well…
If the enslaver eliminates every way of escape from the slave…
There's nothing left for the helot to do,
But to persuade self that,
He does what he's forced to do willingly.
He substitutes devotion for obedience:
The fallacy of devotion!

> He confuses devotion with obedience:
> The fallacy of devotion!
> By this twist, slavery debases the soul:
> As, the freshly minted devotion's a lie…
> The fallacy of devotion.

>> Be erect!
>> For, the earth's fatigued of the impress of your calloused knees.
>> Hold up your chin 'n avow your convictions;
>> Stop bowin' to the caustic power;
>> Power of changin' moods.
>> Withdraw self from this cynical mirage,
>> And, strap your empyrean wings on.
>> For, 'tis better a free soul in a crowded jail,
>> Than a sycophant in a free-street.
>> Be a worshipper of no power

25.4 He Metamorphosed into a Demi-God

(Part 1 of 2)

My able pen journeyed from the North 'n came from the South.
It went huntin' for words to paint a lived history.
Words heavy with love - brilliant as streamin' honey,
And joyous like lovers enterin' an amorous date.
But, my generous stylograph only found a ferocious blade.
A blade with which to tear-down the tyrants' citadel.
So, I talk in allegories – it's gentler.
For, horror's alive - mute but swellin'.

O' this man: M-O-One – a.k.a Footprints;
A nicely grown, well-rounded piece of ill-will!
He who metamorphosed into a demi-god…
His presence filled the land with terror of red 'n taffy.
National pavements were strewn with confetti of baubles.
Patiently 'n unfurlin' like fuchsia funnels breakin'-out of a crab-apple tree;
Citizens embraced the alien notion of continuous livin' of hurt 'n void.
Like starved 'love-machines' thence, they sucked it all.
They thought left undisturbed, light would increase – they were wrong.
They thought he had wisdom because he had power – they were wrong.
His corrupted power made their fathers sire dragon's teeth.
He played upon their fears 'n made their doubts his allies.
As he wore a convincin' mask of peace.
He offered everythin', for offerin' was cheap.
He was ne'er satisfied 'til he was.
Turnin' sons against fathers without their knowledge…

The principles of the Sun's impartial ray's fore'er thrive.
Serenely spinnin' in accordance with Nature's grand scheme;
And, a wind in purpose strong –
It spins against the way it drives.
So, let's hold hands with each other.
Let's hold hands 'n give sunniness to each other.
Aflame with empathies, let each grape to its cluster cling,
And, their elegies sung.
Look deep into self 'n find the grains of hope – 'n sing;
Look deep into self 'n find the grains of strength – 'n endure.
Out of this rape 'n stealth of graft – sing 'n endure.
For, a true gardener moves with a rough sensitivity about under the earth;
Tween the rock 'n shoot;
Ne'er to bruise the hidden fruit.
Be that gardener whose laughter's born-of the love for truth.
Prosper to the apoplex 'n thwart [t]his hatred.

25.5 He Metamorphosed into a Demi-God

(Part 2 of 2)

Every instrument is forsaken by its (own) melody.
The chords of every harp are shredded like a maniac's unmentionables;
And, the singer's voice searches for its singer.
For, the innocent knew nothing as they were too innocent…
The poor heard nothing because they were too impoverished 'n debased…
The rich noticed nothing for they were too busy being rich.
The wisers shrugged their shoulders as they were too wise.
With rational syllables thence,
I sanitize the occult mind 'n silence this promiscuous violence.

Who didn't see imposters join sects of flagellants?
Who didn't see, hear, feel 'n smell citizens tortured 'n executed?
At the hawkish coordination of M-O-One – a.k.a Footprints.
With nil hesitation he shot clean 'n fair,
With a bunch of breasts from either arm.
He turned monuments into taxidermy -
With the help of his four trusted generals:
General Distrust 'n General Fear;
General Greed 'n Major-General Hatred.
Thy smiles hypocrisy - thy words deceit!
A bunch of terrors of truth 'n dart of death.
Who walked in civilian dresses 'n satanically whispered in citizens' ears.
Result: List of the maimed 'n the deads fell through into space.
Etched on a rollin' stone which ne'er rolls.
And, when its shine dulled - its sting faded not.
For, they're wounds which ne'er close.

O' this man: Footprints!
He who described how everywhere he put barns in order - by emptyin' them.
He fed the poor with remnants of what he robbed from the poor.
He declared a fresh dogma:
From now, on doors of beneficent deeds are bolted;
And, every *porte* of sincere work,
Throughout heaven, is slammed shut.
The poetry he invented was incomprehensible:
When he laughed - intellectuals had to laugh,
And when he sobbed - little children died in the streets.
His voice was soft 'n loud – but e'er hoarse.
In loud voice he spoke of great times to come,
And, in soft voice he taught women how to lie-down.
Meanwhile, his back was unquiet as he imagined being screwed.
At death he reversed the moral-accountin' system.
Instead of being held accountable for fatal transgressions,
He metamorphosed into a demi-god.
He (now) plays his dark role with e'er greater spirit.

The more sufferin' there is, the more natural sufferin' appear.
I hear you protest: Who wants to prevent fishes in the sea from getting' wet?
I retort: From a single grain of truth, grow your tree of integrity.
Follow not those who lie in contempt of reality.
Instead, raise to a higher pitch 'n institute harmony within;
And, radiate authentic love for all.

25.6 Wiser to Light a Candle than to Curse Darkness

No metaphor can beautify unfeelin' 'n uncultured mind.
A mind that creates a twirlin' happenstance: an odious dance.
Dance of the hyena - scatterer of excrement.
The one whose spittle 'n drool drip,
From blood-stained crowd of fangs 'n snarlin' lips.

> The scent of blood 'n a weakness in the prey.
> A weakness in the prey's all a wicked needs.
> To enjoy the thrill of pickin' it clean,
> And, leave its bare bones to the winds...
> For, his greediness' second only to that of a false leader.

>> I hear you rightly ask:
>> What's the purpose?
>> What's the true purpose,
>> When cynicism plagues all that breathes?
>> And, I respond:
>> In a world lost to materialistic commercialism -
>> The language of transcendence nourishes harmony.
>> It says not when fire rages, wage war.
>> It counsels to fill your being with the invincibility...
>> Fill self with invincibility of a Deity.
>> And, reach the paradisiacal fantasy...
>> Fantasy of a raisin in the Sun.
>> For, 'tis wiser to light a candle,
>> Than to curse darkness.

25.7 Light the Way for Others

Fake leader's eyes shoot daggers e'en when smilin';
As, he's most fluent with the concepts of deception.
He preaches:
Addition of two negatives turns them positive.
So, he grabs all that soothes his feral ego,
With callous clawed hands.
Then, 'accomplishes' miracles with thunderous splenetic outbursts.

'Executes' miracles with suffocatin' outbursts.
Outbursts that emerge like guano out of a bat's *derrière*.
Leavin' behind a putrid stench of his wretched viscera.
He shamelessly stupefies truth with crafted lies;
And, waters the seeds of life with satanic-acid.
In his presence, fairness loses meanin'.
As whate'er his eye sets-on, attains a dull beauty:
Gnarled Erebus, angel of darkness, envies him.

I hear your protests - again:
What can one person do?
And, I urge you:
Usher self into the stratosphere of true finality:
Raw serenity.
As the greatest gift you can grant humanity's self-transformation;
And, be a candle that consumes itself to light the way for others.

Chapter 26

Greediness

*The avaricious man is barren.
He is like the sandy ground of a desert,
Which sucks in all the rain and dew with greediness.
Sucks in all but yields neither fruitful herbs nor plants,
For the benefit of others.*

~ Zeno of Elea (495 - 425 BC) ~

26.1 Greedy Father has Thieves for Children

Bowin' before the goddess of envious,
Many seem to have tasted from the chalice of covetousness.
As the mystic's favoured much more than the teacher;
And, uncharitable's the moniker for the man of the cloth.

Greediness foams while dreams bleed-out;
And, misery makes its home under the populace's skin.
Covetin' a people with self-stamped ideological warrants.
A contaminated alibi that fattens the flames of false dignity.
As the avarice beat drums chantin' greed.

Shine out your flares 'n birth your golden ripples.
Forge character depth through self-discipline;
And, set your bairns free from this stainin' leaven.
Manifest plainness 'n embrace simplicity.
Have few desires 'n tame egotism.
For, ego has a prideful ferocious appetite for its version of truth.
And, a greedy father has thieves for children!

26.2 Confront the Tainted

Twisted by the eagerness to pursue all that's wrong;
Falsity magnifies the worst twists of fate.
Provides opportunities for breeders of greed;
The birthers of deformities 'n unrefined thoughts.
Thoughts that corrode gates of steel,
Destroyin' the past, present 'n the future.
Makin' the promised-land a mirage.
As a people voyages under a broken sail:
Rollin' left-to-right - pitchin' front-to-rear.

Drownin' in the ocean of deception.
The spitters of the psychosis of brevity,
Aim at the uppermost tree-branch for honey:
With no sweat.
For, they're exquisitely fine-tuned to deceive;
To kill true with their bifurcated tongues.
As they spin their inane songs full of rhythmic conflicts,
Falsehood spews freely from their chartreuse lips,
That eat-clean accrued signs of nefarious acts.
For, counterfeits under inspection they're.

Countenancin' the bakin' of the cake of duplicity,
Isn't less flagitious than ownin' the cake.
Bystandin': equally impeachable!
Thence, listen to the ripplin' inner-streams that flow softly;
Preserve the innate beauty that oozes incessantly;
Along the shores of your interior horizon.
Keep your mind's fair tabernacle pure;
And, glide from star to shinin' star with grace.
Throughout, defend the untainted,
And, confront the tainted.

For, although not everythin' that counts can be counted;
And, not everythin' that can be counted counts;
Integrity counts.
I-n-t-e-g-r-i-t-y counts.

26.3 For Greed All Nature is Little

The greed feels no other pleasure but to acquire.
For greed all nature's little.
His sky stays dark as his vicarious emotion reach his thalamus;
Holdin' inconsequential Namaste grandeur.
As he's the patron saint of finest filigree.
Who strikes deep 'n grows with pernicious roots.
He's a sordid mind - formed of slime 'n filth.

> The greed's a shapeshifter.
> A shapeshifter who lives poor to die rich.
> A master of misplaced generosity.
> Generosity that pauperizes the recipient.
> Generosity that works injuries.
> Injuries that equal exactions of ignoble greed.
> He feels no other pleasure but to acquire.
> Thence, his right gives as his left takes.
> For, what's his, is his, 'n what's yours, is negotiable.

>> These wolves in sheep's clothin' utter saintly words.
>> But, pasted-on wings turn not moles to birds.
>> So, lose not hope in the face of this desolation.
>> Keep your soul clear of wicked thoughts.
>> Walk on the Sun 'n sleep on the Moon.

Chapter 27

Hypocrisy

*Better to die on your feet,
Than to live on your knees.*

~ Aeschylus (525 – 456 BC) ~

27.1 Ripples of Pomp and Inconsistencies

What a time!
A time when the dealer in the bodies of men,
Pampers the pulpit with his bloody diamond.
When the pulpit covers the dealer's infernal business,
With a deific garb.
Twin-angels of opacity, they're.
Dark angels who lie with sincerity;
And, crucify light to keep darkness alive.
As they're hypocrites even when asleep.
Their life-dance's a pathetic display of imbecilic prancin',
Birthin' multitudinous ripples of inconsistencies.

What a time!
A time when hyenas of hate suckle the younglings of men;
And, jackals of hypocrisy pimp their mothers' broken hearts.
To stay atop,
They drown those beneath.
As they're serpents who ne'er play fair.
They're magi whose spell's manipulation.
As their preachin' ne'er reach their ears;
And, possess knowledge that ne'er reach their souls.
Provokin' ripples of pomp 'n inconsistencies.

What a time!
A time when the cart pleads for progress to a reluctant horse.
When youth look to demigods of ignorance for hope.
Wherefore goddess of goodness decrees:
Peter-out these ripples!
Be who you ought to be!
Aspire for wellness that needs no audience.
Let your innate vicomtesse dribble.

Let it dribble effortlessly from your heart.
As nature's vividly aware of the iron hand.
Iron hand underneath your velvet-mitts.
For, hypocritical humility's the highest form of lyin'.
And, honest arrogance's the lowest form of egoic-promotion.
O' dear, cripple these ripples of pomp 'n inconsistencies!

27.2 I'll Charm

I birth gray thoughts.
So, I confess: I'll charm you 'til the cat looms larger than the lion;
Till the Higher wields the Lower 'n the Lower the Higher.
I'll caress you good 'til you hear with your eyes 'n see with your ears.
But, I hear the reticence that bids,
The dreamer abandon his (unmet) dream.
But, I'll charm…

'Tis time to write our collective will…
To castrate these Monsters:
Lovers of enemy's clipped ears.
Beasts whose meanings clearer,
Than the Egyptian Amun aroused from slumber.
Bêtes who confuse the brightness of moon,
With the prosaic light of Sun.
As they're excruciatingly strong in their stale thoughts;
And, content to live where life began.
But, in thought 'n act - in soul 'n sense -
I'll [still] charm…

…And the charmin' commences…
Boundless inward - boundless outward.
Down with diffidence!
Let's set the feet above the brain;
And, let the brain be the feet.
Let's paint their dull decrepitude(s) with the livin' hues of Nature…
Let's set their juvenile fantasies wallowin' in the troughs of Zolaism…
Let's rip their testy delirium open - strip 'em bare.

Naked - let 'em stare.
Lets shove their ruins down their leakin' malodorous buttholes!
…And, the cat shall be the lion 'n the lion the cat…
…The Higher shall be the Lower 'n the Lower the Higher…
…And, we shall all hear with our eyes 'n see with our ears…

I hear [again] the reticence that bids,
The dreamer abandon his (noble) dream…
And dolorously, Amun slumbers – *encore*!

27.3 I'll Charm: A Clarion Call

Many read *I'll Charm*.
Many commented on *I'll Charm*.
Many questioned *I'll Charm's* spirit.
I proffer: *I'll Charm's* about life – in *toto*.

> *I'll Charm's* a clarion call - for you.
> A call to nurture your inner world.
> By explorin' your shinin' hours towards self-fulfilment;
> And, cultivatin' harmony in your wheel of life.
> A call to experience the essence of life.
> By being aware of your innate power,
> And, unfoldin' the truth of your soul.
> …Without toleratin' insolence 'n patchiness…

> *I'll Charm's* a clarion call - for all.
> A collective call to be a life-affirmin' being.
> A being free of (sub)conscious mindsets.
> A being who resets inner-drive;
> To pursue vibrant love-inspired relationships.
> For, today's tomorrow's yesterday.
> So, *I'll Charm* directs us to feel;
> And, fill life with mindfulness!

Chapter 28

Mediocrity

When obvious that the goals are unreachable.
The mediocre adjusts the goals;
While the wiser adjusts the action steps.

~ Confucius (551 – 479 BC) ~

28.1 Shallowness Conceals a Delayed Defeat

Doubt not:
Grapes of wrath birth mirth filled grapes;
But, lemmings enact bellyachin' absurdities.

A refined General opts for no war;
As, deep waters are calm.
But, unwiser can (ne'er) know.
So, help him revert to the original divine dream.

How so?
'Tis a collective onus,
To dismantle this hamlet of mediocrity.
As shallowness conceals a delayed defeat.

28.2 Mediocrity Sedates and Blinds

Mediocrity sedates mind.
As 'tis a pernicious 'n insidious slayer.
A philistine of civility,
That slows the clock to maintain the status quo.
But, some are born mediocre,
While others achieve mediocrity.

Mediocrity blinds the pineal eye.
A veritable hollowness with no inside but gold-dust outline.
Dust that evanesces under the wind -
In an instant...
But, some are born mediocre,
While others achieve mediocrity.

Some are born mediocre.
Some achieve mediocrity.
Some have mediocrity thrust upon them.
Have encountered some who had been all three.
They're simultaneously prisoners 'n guards.
With keys to escape in their palms.
But, they prefer to stay in their self-made congenial prisons.
They force squares into circular places;
And, change what ought to remain unchanged.
Like a prismatic medium, they reflect unsober elements,
Actively effusin' fungi fumes.
They aren't only mediocre –
They're mediocrity!

28.3 Return - Free of Mediocrity

To learn what's in life's store,
You must open each door.
In the process, mediocrity's the cripplin' malady.
Better rest - if you must.
Make mistakes along the way.
Learn from them…
Be afraid not – of the new;
Better even, live not in the past
Take each moment as if it were your last.
Remember though:
First step's the hardest travelled mile.

> Set your goals high.
> But, be kind to self.
> Be sincere in your deeds.
> Respect those you meet in the flight of life.
> And, treat them as you wish they would you;
> With no room for mediocrity.
>
> > Do your thing with utmost contentment;
> > No room for resentment.
> > So, if you must go - go for a while.
> > And, when you return,
> > Return with a smile –
> > Free of mediocrity.

Chapter 29

Prejudice

Since we are not yet fully comfortable with the idea that,
People from the next village are as human as ourselves;
It is presumptuous in the extreme,
To suppose we could ever look at sociable,
Tool-making creatures from other evolutionary paths and see not beasts,
But brothers, not rivals,
But fellow pilgrims journeying to the shrine of intelligence...
The difference is not in the creature judged,
But in the creature judging.

~ Demosthenes (384 – 322 BC) ~

And,

Prejudice cannot see the things that are;
Because it is always looking for things that are not.

~ Mark Twain (1835 – 1910 AD) ~

29.1 Bigotry Turns You into a Hope Slayer

I dreamt of a pleasant land,
Where empathy free flows.
Beyond the dreamland, heartrendingly,
The sententious lesson to her intransigently continues…
She's taught: E'ery violence that you experience,
Is a fruit of the length of your skirt.
'Tis the product of the plunge of your blouse-line.
E'ery lurkin' danger meted upon you, is the sum of your faults.
For, when an egoic man incites himself to drown,
'Tis the water's fault…
What a folly!

In these Ziegfeld Follies he joyously paints a naked woman,
Then labels the painting vanity.
He chastises the very nakedness he authored.
Unapologetically thus, I scream his name,
Swallowin' all syllables the wrong way.
To warn: Misogynist's bilious worldview reeks repugnance ignorance.
But, only persistence ignorance is ill faith.
For, 'tis oafish, vacuous and numb;
Defensive with nothing worth defendin'.

To misogynist: Bigotry turns you into a hope slayer.
And, with a logic of indisputability, know as follows:
There's no happy ending in subjugation.
To women: Be proud 'n brave.
Ferociously fight for your spot at the head of the table.
Firmly fix your eyes on the Moon 'n your feet on Earth.
To humanity: Wear anti-sexism 'n anti-misogyny spray,
For purification commences in the soul.

29.2 Moon wouldn't Sparkle without Darkness

They hellishly ripped the innocent swellin' of her womb;
With a butcher's knife - to save time 'n energy.
Then, stuck its eyes onto their earlobes,
Like Egyptian jewellery.
So biased, none of us know her – Sharon(g) or Sharin(g)!

To some, she shared the intangibles – happiness, joy, love…
To the self-declared puritans, she shared the tangibles – her body…
Thence, they christen her accordingly:
A woman of ill-repute.
One who upsets the natural order.
A loose woman on the loose.
In this cacophony of folly,
We can't see ourselves through the other.
For we savour schadenfreude.

O' brother, find no fault with the limpin' sister.
For, there may be tacks in her shoes.
O' sister, sneer not at the fallen brother.
For, you have tasted not the blow that caused the stumble.
I hear you maniacally yell:
I'm strong!
I maintain regardless:
If Sharon(g)'s blows, were dealt unto you;
In the selfsame way…
You'll stagger, too.
So, pelt her with no unsavoury words.
Unless your underthings are stainless.
For, the moon wouldn't sparkle without darkness.

29.3 Lies are Told and Legends Made

Lies are told 'n legends made.
But, the Black Philosopher knows:
Phoenix rises unafraid.
For, what's goin' on;
Is goin' on.
As lies are told 'n legends made.

>   Lies are told 'n legends made.
>   Drownin' all in fused images.
>   Drownin' in fused images beneath my pain thence,
>   I gaze at the world,
>   Through a fenced-off gnarly narrow space.
>   A space assigned to me at conception.
>   I look at the world,
>   From awakenin' eyes in a racialized face…
>   And, I know:
>   These walls of racism shall collapse!
>   I hear your protests: How so?
>   As lies are told 'n legends made.

>   >   O' dear reader - lies are told 'n legends made.
>   >   But, I had the honour of learnin' from the best - you.
>   >   Learnin' of the importance of boldly takin' e'ery step,
>   >   With courage 'n intent.
>   >   And, I know:
>   >   These walls of racism shall collapse!
>   >   As lies collapse 'n legends rise.

29.4 Racism can and Must be Defeated

Sun's shinin' 'n birds are chirpin'.
Winds are singin' 'n waves are dancin'.
The morning harmony's perfect.
Suddenly, rumblin' creeps in painful slowness.
Dimmin' the sun 'n drownin' the birds;
Turnin' the sweetness of the morning freshness into a stench of injustice.

Natch, I can't make you see what I see,
With your blinders on.
I can't make you hear what I hear,
With your paddin' on.
Take-off the blinkers from your eyes 'n see the tears.
Tears of blood throbbin' through slitted veins.
Take-off the waddin' from your ears 'n hear the cries of pain.
Cries whose intensity 'n rhythm changes not.
As humanity struggles with the ghosts of its past – hatred;
And the burdens of its present – racism;
Tryin' to find its way to the future – harmony.

O' humanity,
I express views that aren't unheard by sayin':
Racism has a heart,
But arteries full of cruelty 'n death.
Racism has a mind,
But intellect of savagery 'n vile ideology.
For, I see the sickly color of racism not e'ery other day;
But e'ery minute of the day.
As prejudice can't be hidden;
And, the axe forgets, but the tree remembers.
I smell the fetid smell of racism e'ery minute of the day.

When people aren't hired because of skin pigments.
I feel the burnin' sensation of racism e'ery minute of the day.
When people are slaughtered because of their skin color.
I hear the coarse voice of racism not e'ery other day;
But, e'ery minute of the day.
For, racism lurks in the air – embedded in [all] social systems:
Courthouses, governments, schools, public places …
Ready to maim 'n kill.

Children are born free of bigotry 'n hate.
With their pure lovin' ways – they're taught ugliness.
So, let's plant seeds that bear fruits of hope.
By replacin' ignorance with knowledge 'n apathy with empathy.
By dissentin' from indifference 'n hatred.
Let's disarm the ghosts of humanity's past – hatred;
And, the burdens of its present – racism.
For, racism can 'n must be defeated.
Be part of the light!

29.5 Live for Today and Hope for Tomorrow

Knee on the neck.
...on the neck – dead!
The wind blows, the waves break.
Thunder sounds - flash of frightenin' light;
Children scream - screams of fright.
Lone firefly flies by - gone!
'Tis dark – moonless sky;
No light - starless sky.
What a wrenchin' pain!

Here comes the wonder that separates the stars:
The root of roots;
The sap of tree of life – a new dawn.
In the pulse of this novel dawn,
Lift up your heart…
Have the grace to look into the *Other's* eyes,
And say simply:
I see you - I hear you.
For, in the pulse of this fresh dawn,
Each hour holds a new beginnin'.
As the horizon leans forward,
Offerin' you space to place unsullied steps of change.
And, touch the World.
So, keep the desire to go forward – one bold baby-step at a time.
For, however long the night, the dawn shall break.

O' dear, ne'er cease dreamin',
Ne'er stop being amazed by small wonders of life;
And, ne'er tire of buildin' bridges.
For, the World has just been born:
The best race hasn't been run;

And, the best score hasn't been made.
So, ne'er stop shinin' in your own way;
And, ne'er forget, brighter tomorrows are e'er near.
For, the World's young:
The best verse hasn't been rhymed;
And, the best tune hasn't been played.

Learn from yesterday;
But, live for today 'n hope for tomorrow.
Accept finite disappointment but harbor infinite hope.
Like a willow, thence, bend but break not.
For, 'tis e'er better beyond the horizon.
As there's no night that can defeat sunup;
And, no challenge that can defeat hope.
For, hope's a walkin' dream.
So, give rebirth to your original dream;
Flick your light back on,
Shine it brighter than e'er;
And, touch the World.
For, tears shed for another's a sign of an empyrean heart.

29.6 Let Your Voice be Heard

Today,
I think of two innocent souls…
Souls whose girlhood has been replaced with tears 'n fear;
Disbelief 'n dread.
By the raider of innocence –
A fake mathematics teacher.
A teacher who cuts deep 'n wide.

> *Aujourd'hui,*
> I think of the stain 'n stink of stolen childhood:
> Stain 'n stink that linger – forever.
> I think of the betrayal 'n disgust that remain:
> Betrayal 'n disgust of stolen innocence – forever.

>> *Leo,*
>> I tell the two innocent girls:
>> Be silent statistics not.
>> Let your voice be heard –
>> 'Tshall be heard.
>> Keep your eyes heavenward;
>> And, your footin' earthward.
>> May the road rise up to meet you;
>> And, may the wind be at your back.

29.7 I Speak for the Unborn

Despite its wrenchin' pain, history cannot be un-lived.
And, if faced with courage, it needs be re-lived not.
Today however, Iris verna blooms;
But, the caged bird sings no more.
For, the knee's on his throat –
Unceasingly with unflaggin' resolve.

So, I speak for the unseen:
The desperate who dies expensively.
I speak for the unborn:
The enlightened who salute rainbows 'n butterflies.
For I know, they'd be more or less mad for similar reasons.

O' dear reader,
I had the privilege of observin',
Your direct 'n respectable strides...
As direct 'n self-acceptin' as a lion in Afrikan Savannah.
So, I (now) look at the world,
From awakenin' eyes in a racialized face.
And, I know: humanity shall reign!
For, you're the window: You let light in.
For, you're the mirror: You reflect the light of love.
Thus, I declare: this wonderin' is short-lived.
As, with genuine love,
Souls disfigured by hatred can be healed.

29.8 Someone has to Sever this Chain

A mule turnin' a millstone isn't tryin' to press oil.
Rather, he's fleein' the blow just struck;
And, hopin' to avoid the next blow.
For similar reasons,
The slave follows slave master's rules not to be a better slave,
Rather, he's tryin' to ease dull pain,
He turns the oppressive millstone;
To ease the numbin' social pain;
The pain of the unfeelin' (wo)man of poisoned dreams.
Yes: I've swum in those poisoned waters – waters of racism;
And, my tears begot no sense of release.

I've travelled that poisoned road – road of racism.
A road of turns 'n turns.
On e'ery turn,
Comes more pain than at the last turn.
E'ery step I took – more pain I earned…
At each turn,
The deadened (wo)man of poisoned dreams signalled for my surrender.
At each signal,
I threw up my flag of non-surrender.
But, each blow left a deep gash.
A deep gash that constantly reopens - never able to heal.
Scars on my eyes 'n cicatrices in my heart tell the tale.
The tale of the deep slashes in my soul.
A soul wanderin' through the poisoned wilderness –
Wilderness of racism.

Oh yeah - I've danced through that poisoned dance – dance of racism;

And, my tears brought no sense of repose.
But today,
I throw up my flag of non-surrender – again.
For, I'm interested in the story –
The story of the unfeelin' (wo)man of poisoned dreams.
And, someone has to sever this chain of hatred.
For, cheapenin' the lives of some,
Cheapens the lives of all.
As, racism cheapens life -
Racism cheapens humanity.

29.9 Let the Caller and the Called merge

If your ship's of 'impure' peel – set not to their shore.
In your presence - they wish you well.
In your absence - they kill your dream.
They're parasitic with poison-laced tongues.
They cause pain while pleadin' the law to cover their twisted deeds.
They breathe 'n breed hatred…
For, they're hate.
Unified, let's not showcase their fetid look.
Let's not give racism a stage.

***

O' you of the receivin' end…
O' you of oddly shaped wings…
The axe forgets - the tree forgets not.
But, the moment's here:
The moment to join the nightingale in the garden;
The moment to taste sugar with the soul-parrot;
The moment to awaken to the true path;
And, give your soul a glass of love.
So, let the tree birds fill the air with songs.
For, on an alchemist' touch,
Copper loses its copperness;
And, in spring,
Seeds lose their seedness.
So, let the caller 'n the called merge.
For, in the valley of my dreams I see hate dissolve,
If we reject all that smells like team ignorance.

O' you of the receivin' end...
The axe forgets - the tree forgets not.
But, kindliness makes bitter things sweet;
With love dregs settle into clarity;
And, with fairness sufferin' ceases.
...If there is no healin' of ill feelings,
There will be less ill will,
So, free your mind of ill will.
Dig deeper than deep 'n forgive all.
Not because they deserve your forgiveness;
But because you deserve sanity.
And, holdin' onto anger,
Is like graspin' hot coal with the intent of throwin' it at the other;
You get burned!

O' you of the receivin' end...
The axe forgets - the tree forgets not.
But, e'ery time you forgive - the universe changes;
E'ery time you touch a life - humanity changes.
So, dig deeper than deep;
And, react not with bitterness.
Instead, transform your sufferin' into a creative force.
For, that open wound allows light to enter you.
So, love as if there'll be no morrow;
And, if morrow appears - love again.

O' you of oddly shaped wings...
The axe forgets - the tree forgets not.
So, clean the mud 'n straw – in your soul.
Let the humane mirror be revealed.
For, till the juice ferments, it isn't wine.
Genuinely wrestle with your demons of biasness;
Wrestle with your succubus of prejudice;

And, your angels will sing your humane song.
Overcome your diabolical resentments against those unlike you;
And proclaim your freshness 'n purity.
Be…
Be just…
Be kind…
Be honest…
Be loveable…
And, let the caller 'n the called merge.

Chapter 30

Hatred

*No one is born hating another person,
Because of the colour of his skin,
Or his background, or his religion.
People must learn to hate,
And if they can learn to hate,
They can be taught to love.
For love comes more naturally,
To the human heart than it's opposite.*

~ Nelson Mandela (1918 – 2013 AD) ~

30.1 Let Doves of Love Take on Wings

O' humanity,
Listen with eye of mind.
Borrow 'n build upon love.
Turn not your anger into hate.
For, hate destroys.

Hear me humanity,
Love prevails under the dark clouds of evil.
For, even a lone star shinin' on an overcast night,
Shines hope bright.

O' humanity,
Let the doves of love take on wings,
Let the spirit of *ubuntu* endure!

30.2 Beautiful Things Ask for no Attention

How can I participate in my life again?
How can I get out of bed unaided again?
How can I play with my kids again?
He incessantly posed loudly.

The Army of Nothings spout 'n spit at him.
To feel stronger - they told him he's weak.
To feel prettier - they proclaimed him ugly.
To feel smarter - they declared him dumb.
For, they pleasure in others' pain;
As their minds are dull 'n hearts pitch-dark.
His soul cried for peace, but received carnage 'n hate.

O' this man!
He had a chance to be ruined in his transient existence.
He chose self-reflection.
Thus, like a street dancer,
He shone in all directions.
He found the rhythm of infinite possibilities within self.
He re-climbed the mountain not to be seen;
But, to see the world.
For, beautiful things ask for no attention.

30.3 Let the Spirit of Humanity Endure

Ubuntu judders - humanity shudders.
As history repeats its saga of barbarism.
Thunderous bang;
Shrapnel ignominiously blossom;
Dancin' through innocent flesh.
In a precedented opera of hate.
In a shameless opera of death.

> O' sick opera…
> Opera founded on distortions of faith 'n fanatic fervour.
> Orchestrated by horrendous maniacs with twisted souls;
> And, intolerant minds cleansed of reason.
> Executed by pitiful lunatics blinded by ignorance.
> Whose cold reptilian brains bear the hallmark,
> Of barbarousness concealed in human flesh;
> And, souls that slither like venomous rapists.
> Rapists who feed on the virginal innocence of the other.
> As horror 'n hatred is their *raison d'être*.

>> To the innocent targets whose lives ceased:
>> May your souls find instant peace.
>> As, you lived for love 'n parted with love.
>> And, when you died, so did a part of humanity.
>> To those who left the comfort of their homes,
>> To confront the devil incarnate:
>> Embodiment of goodness you remain.
>> To the rest: Value those you meet;
>> And, refuse hate by renouncin' hatred.

30.4 Greatness Begins in Our Minds

Hatred-based challenges are the doorway to new sight:
They wake our light!
Dark challenges are the unanswered knock on the door:
They announce the need to push harder.

They teach us 'n remind us,
That nature responds to the octaves of our vibration.
She pulsates within the wavelength of our pendulum.
Swingin' circumspectively overly around us.

Ergo, we can do the impossible,
As we carry a seed of greatness.
A seed that only need to be sowed in a fertile ground.
Let your inner-self lead - breathe it in;
And, bring your magic to life.
For, greatness begins in our minds.

Chapter 31

Pandemic

Be safe,
Be smart,
Be kind.

~ Tedros Ghebreyesus (WHO Director General, 2020) ~

31.1 Old Nick has Licked…

Old Nick has licked the promised-land – *encore une fois*!
With his dull tendrils,
Tendrils as loathsome as fat Cerberus,
He reaches, claws, twiddles, twists…
Once we drop our guard.

Ejaculated dusts of terror onto our lips 'n lungs.
As we took the third-step before the second;
And, skipped cleansin' after release.
In this endless game of correction of errors:
Pain brings forth pain;
'Til souls become soulless.
As the dancer of death trundles the globe,
Gassin' the bodies of the weak like Hiroshima heat,
And, gobblin' all that nourishes hope.
Leavin' us coughin' 'n hackin';
Tryin' 'n tryin' to breathe;
As we can chew no-more without coughin' –
Like a pack of seals.

O' yeah: When your back wobbles;
And, your eyes blurred…
When your tongue's furred;
And, your tonsils squeak…
When your head's abuzz;
And, arsehole leaks…
Then, you've been licked –
You got it: *Convid-19 o.k.a Corona*.

31.2 Covid-19 o.k.a Crorona

Horrid Corona!
You've wrecked social lives.
Prevented lovers from kissin'.
Made all to bathe in steamin' vinegared water at ungodly hours.
You've thieved loved ones,
Bringin' pain(s) to many hearts.
For, this bleedin' has no bias:
From Wuhan to Codogno – you devoured all.

But, there's no good fight without a worthy opponent:
What's strength without pain?
What's life without death?
Indeed, Epicurus (341 - 270 BC) maintains:
Death's a part of life.
But, who wants to die?
Seneca (4 BC – 65 AD) retorts:
E'en the infirm lives for morrow.

So, stand in the art of livin'.
Live in the art of strength 'n courage…
An art pursued by those who stand in the light of love -
Unafraid to keep the lights shinin' contra-Corona.
By posin' questions 'n findin' answers.
Be forewarned though:
When you teach all, you must pay self.
And, that's the beauty of servin' humanity.
Ergo, midwife the art of tenacity 'n community.
For, the sure-fire way to hang Corona's together.
By holdin' on to our unifyin' ribbons of hope,

And banners of humanity.
United thence, let's glow 'n come 'n go - flash on flush.
For, pure acetylene - virgin – attended by Cherubim,
We remain!

31.3 Let's Become Better for Each Other

The woods are dark 'n deep;
But, I've promises to keep;
And, miles to kill before I sleep.
So, I cleared my forest yesterday…
Now, I see the forest through the trees;
And, the moon through the stars.
No longer have to climb up on my roof,
To see things unseen yesterday.
Through the cleared forest, I see a multitude;
A people who switch the channel,
To avoid seein' filled-up ICU beds.
I see them lickin' the skunky-butt of their fake hero:
He who engages Covid-19 for one-on-one contest.

> O' believers of the orange-headed hoaxer:
> He who walks around bare-chested,
> With a phoney superhero aura.
> He who engages Covid-19 for a buffoonish combat…
> Listen to facts.
> Take the path of light 'n enlightenment,
> Embrace the path of love 'n kindness.
> Kiss your center 'n radiate positive vibration for humanity-sake.
> And, help win this messy fight – Coronavirus fight.

>> Dear humanity, in the midst of this historic menace,
>> Dyin' is easy 'n livin' is hard.
>> So, let's collectively fight this horrific fight.
>> Abide by health dictates:
>> Self-isolate 'n keep a decent distance;
>> Sanitize 'n mask-it.

And, save self 'n your family.
Throughout, smile at the Sun,
And break the rusty jaws of Covid-19.
For, a singular burst of cosmic glow points to a splendid future.
So, embraced in deep endearment,
Let's overcome Corona's ugliness
Once dead, may we ne'er take for granted:
A handshake with a stranger 'n coffee with a friend.
Once exterminated, may we become who we ought to be:
Better for each other.
For, we're in this together!

31.4 Self-isolate, Rub and Wipe this Monster

Fire's ragin' past borders - from Auckland to Denver.
Horrendous static's in the air - from Ottawa to Pretoria.
Makin' humanity confuse certainty with uncertainty.
As old Nick licks humanity.
With this riptide lick,
Gradual darkness creeps inch-by-inch;
As constant drip-drip gnaws you in-out.
Your thirst for clarity 'n purity stifles;
As your interior shifts on slow motion.
Your senses fluctuate 'n blur;
As your leaky-leaky gut takes control.
Your inner pipin' corrodes,
Makin' you sneeze in evens 'n cough in odds;
And, singin' in the toilet counts as a talent.
By Sunup your heavy eyelids know not if its dusk or dawn.
So, self-isolate, take a duster;
Rub 'n wipe this monster.

Veridical deal:
Humanity's rainin' from inside.
For, this epizootic's a castor oil drippin' onto rangin' fire;
A grain of sand inward an oyster shell - that sinks hope.
O' this Corona-monster pretty nice not.
But, it can rain fore'er not.
The sunshine's comin'.
United thence,
Let's work for a common cause - humanity.
So, self-isolate, take a duster;
Rub 'n wipe this monster.

Lift each other 'n sing,

'Til Earth 'n Heaven ring.
Ring with the harmony of benevolence;
And, rejoice to the listenin' skies.
Throughout, take a deep breath of the Universe.
And, admire her elegancy at each Sun born.
Ergo, like moon kissin' the night-sky,
Illuminate the majesty of the dark-sky,
And, bring the beauty of e'ery star alive.
For, together we can get out of this darkness.
Get out without leavin' dark marks on the 'other'.
We can surmount this strain.
Surmount this strain without puttin' stain on others.
So, self-isolate, take a duster;
Rub 'n wipe this monster.

31.5 Let Every Life Saved Make You Humbler

Humanity's being danced.
Not the nice self-conscious shuffle dance;
But the shakin' bones dance.
The dance that tears scabs open 'n strips us off our casings.
With a corrosive mind of its own;
And, its flames lickin' from all directions…
The unblinkin' *Tomb Stalker* skulks near 'n far;
Devourin' lives by thousands.
Leavin' a putrid night of fallen-bodies 'n bare-bones.

Through this direful darkness:
As the moon faded into an impossible sliver of light;
And, stars struggled through the dense sheets of clouds;
Your voices got clearer.
Gowned, gloved 'n masked - on a fire 'n brimstone mission;
You dived in 'n took the hit for us all.
You strode deeper into the beast's, read Covid-19, fiefdom.
Determined to do what you do best: Save lives from the beast.
A beast whose heart burns with contagious annihilation…
Determined to free humanity from this forlorn mire…
Collectively, you're real-life heroes.

O' front-liners: Stand tall!
O' essential-workers: Walk tall!
As I bow to you one 'n all.
For, you're life savers to many 'n heroes to all.
Dōmo arigatō gozaimashita for the care given;
And, for that will come to be.
Let e'ery life lost make you stronger;
And, e'ery life saved make you humbler.
May pure grace unstintingly rain upon y'all.

Chapter 32

Death

The universe is the harmony of opposites:
There's no water without fire,
There's no female with no male,
There's no night without day,
There is no sun without the moon...
There is no good without evil!

To know the thrill of health,
One must first be ill.

Ying-Yang captures life.
As white 'n black embraces each other:
Inside the white there's a black;
In death there's life.

32.1 Nature passes away to be revivified

Nature has feelings.
In silence she speaks happiness beyond the reach of a poet.
But, her decay's the green life of change:
She passes away to be revivified.
As, one would enjoy not the Sun if it ne'er rained;
One would yearn not for light if there were no darkness.
And, life would be meaningless without death.
Death clears out the old to make way for the new.
'Tis not extinguishin' the light;
But, lightin' the lamp just before dawn.
For, the day we fear as our last,
Is the birthday of eternity.

We'd smile 'n wait in contentment if only we could:
See the splendour of their new found land;
Know the reason why they were called home;
Hear the welcome they receive,
From old familiar voices all so dear.
For, there's a plan far magnificent than the known;
A landscape far splendid than the visible;
And, a haven for the souls: a rebirth.
The soul's hampered not by time or space –
'Tis immortality.
As one mixes with the elements - irreversibly.
To be a kin to the insensible rock;
And, the sluggish clod, which the rude swain treads upon.

To the parted: Your branches grew brightly –
Full of sap 'n silver dew;
Birds gather nightly beneath your shelter.
Bees make rounds around your nectary flowers.

Unannounced, the god of darkness plucked the golden blossom;
Stripped-off the foliage in its pride…
But, into our hearts flowed life's restorin' tide:
Infinity's life immortal.
For those who rejoice, time's brief;
And, for those who love, time's eternity.
So, to the livin': break in the Sun 'til the Sun breaks down,
And, the angel of death shall have no dominion.

32.2 I Hold up My Lamp to Light Your Way

To friends above, from a friend below...
The indignant ghost's riven, but wafts pæan of times of yore.
Slipped the earthly-surly bonds;
You danced sunward through the footless halls of air;
On laughter-silvered wings with easy grace.
But, when a great tree falls,
Rocks shudder 'n beasts recoil into quietude.
When a (great) soul falls,
Air becomes sterile 'n eyes see with a hurtful clarity.
When that which drew from out the boundless deep (re)turns home.
Memories are sharpened 'n souls are wizened.
So, with your new seraphic wings, go meet *The Pilot* – fearlessly.

As the train of life winds 'n turns;
The cadence of your life songs will live-on:
All in one mighty livin' sepulchre.
We bow unto you like the vales stretchin' in pensive peacefulness;
Like venerable rivers snakin' in majesty, and
Uncomplainin' brooks that green the meadows.
For, now you know what we learn:
'Tis no demise – 'tis immortality.
Like the lovely Sun,
Only when we set in the west can we rise in the east.
So, sing your songs, 'n dance your dances,
Like heroes (re)turnin' home – to meet *The Pilot*.

One with inner courage dares to live;
One with outward courage dares to die.
You had inner-outward courage.

With face lit with delight 'n gratitude thence,
I say: So fine a time!
I bow to you 'n hold up my humble lamp to light your way.

32.3 Unexpected Departure

Pain so deep-down-inside.
So deep it can't be captured in words.
Pain that touches the toe ascendin' to the ceilin'.
That's the pain we feel today.
For, your unexpected departure was a real hit.

> The change you made in the world;
> Can't be gainsaid.
> Day 'n night, a hero you remain.
> For, you walked in many people's shoes.
> You taught us:
> Without experimentation - we become static.
> You experimented.
> Without the willingness to ask questions - we become repetitive.
> You questioned.
> Without the inclination to try new things - we become moribund.
> You tried novel things.
>
>> Your charisma;
>> Your smile;
>> Your humility; and,
>> Your big heart…
>> Made each day new.
>> For, you were true to the call.
>> *Sayonara!*
>>
>> *[In memory of a good friend]*

32.4 Melody of a Lovely Song

No goodbye uttered - none was needed.
The Principal Designer broke our hearts – *encore une fois*;
To prove He harvests the best.
Grasping your departure was like reachin' for the stars.
A task that was drainin' 'n overbearin';
A suffocating emotional bag.
Like the sugar in burning tea, I knew not what to taste.
But now stars are closer 'n the light of understandin' is brighter.
Ergo, I reach for reality strain-free 'n I comprehend it was time:
Fate took hold!

Dearest 'One', here're my partin' words:
Melody of a lovely song, you're;
And, no flint was in vain on the path you trod.
Today, I hear your laughter 'n your voice.
I remember your smile like I have no choice.
For, like a blazin' fire - you radiated warmth.
Like a freshly cut diamond - you shone 'n sparkled.
Like a godly magnet – you attracted love.
With your courage 'n wisdom - you inspired.
Thus, though out of sight, you remain in our minds.
As we feel you with every breath.
'Til we meet, remain you:
Ego-less, elegant, humble, lovely, funny…
And, enjoy the sunshine in the rain dear 'One'.
You are treasured!

The comfort of having a friend may be taken away;
But, not that of havin' had one – we had 'One'.
So, let's smile for 'One' lived good.
Let's open eyes 'n appreciate what 'One' left.

Let's open ears 'n embrace 'One's' echo whisperin' softly heaven-down-ward.
Let's cherish 'One's' memory 'n enable it shine-on.
By doing what she did best:
Loving 'n being kind to others.
Thence, as we gaze with gladness upon 'One's' friendship,
Let's say in unison:
Peace be upon you dear 'One'…
And leave the rest to Him 'n His able palms.

[In memory of an authentic friend]

32.5 Mama Leah Dear

There's no endin' to Mama Leah's story,
A new chapter has begun
A chapter full of grace 'n glory.
Mama has been called home,
For, He chooses only the best.
Yes, she's physically not with us.
But, in our hearts she resides.
In our heart she'll remain for eternity.

Mama Leah was an icon of love 'n a beacon of peace,
An exemplar of unity 'n a symbol of strength.
She saw the light in everyone 'n gave with no regrets.
As she loved unconditionally.
When no one else would listen, in her we confided.
When we told her of our mistakes, she nodded sayin':
So have we all.
She reminded us:
The key to success' learning from our mistakes.
Let's all take this as a key lesson from Mama Leah.
A lesson from one whose love knew no boundaries.

Mama, we think of you in silence.
We speak your name for all to hear.
We look at your photographs to see your smile.
As your memory's our keepsake - with which we'll ne'er part.
He has you in his keepin' - we have you in our hearts.
Love you Mama!

32.6 Rest in Peace Dave Dear

No words we write could e'er say
How sad 'n empty our feelings are;
As the Angels dropped for Dave Senior;
Much sooner than anyone of us knew.

> To those who knew Dave,
> May your tormented minds be clear 'n calm.
> May your tender hearts be warm, as Dave knew.
> Brave the bitter grief that comes 'n try to understand
> Know now, Dave's in a better place.
> No more hurt 'n no more pain shall he face.
> As he's watchin' o'er us!

>> Dave dear,
>> For all our love 'n memories;
>> We'll hold fore'er near 'n dear.
>> As you watch o'er us!

32.7 Dear Mama…

Dear mama…,
If I could have just one more day…
Only one more day,
A day to spend every glorious moment with you.
Recallin' memories with you dear mama…

If I could have just one more day…
Just one more day;
Where the tears I'm sheddin' only fall in bliss.
So many things I'd tell you;
How grateful I would be to,
Have just one more day with you mama.

If I could have just one more day…
But, *The Maker* had better plans for you mama…
So, the day came 'n the Sun began to set…
A million times I'd let you know dear mama:
Never will I forget,
The heart of gold you left behind,
As you enter the heaven's gate;
To meet *The Heaven Owner* –
The Principal Maker.

32.8 We Heard the Thunderclap as You Fell

Dearest brother, from Antares to Canopus,
We heard the thunderclap.
The thunder as you fell back-head first;
Onto the hard concrete of your equal opportunity.
As sixteen explosive bullet's perforated your fresh,
Like push pins holdin' up a connect the dots map of Africa.
According you no time to hit the floor with dignity,
The bullet's instantly smoked you into spirit.
Your innocent blood ran red somewhere only known to the brutish police.
At the limits of Karura Forest,
You were left as a murderer's masterpiece.
To be found face-down,
Blooded 'n divided at waist – dead.
Certainly, Angels sang songs of protest while you bled.
I wanted not you to go away quietly either…
I'll reveal what happened:
A promise to an aging mother, I made.

Your killin' wasn't a sudden outburst of uncontrolled fury;
Not unspeakable brutality of an insane mob.
'Twas the deliberation of psychopaths who practice unwritten law;
Law that justifies killin' the innocent for pleasure.
For, they've birthright to rape 'n accumulate.
As the brutes clad in khaki strut as slaves of political goons.
O' goodliness, how this anguish was orchestrated by the isles' prince.
The creature of the old born in the sea fortress speakin' the language of dragons.
He who became the embodiment of the knighthood,

With his destiny chiselled on stone.

O' dear, we're drownin' in this cacophony of folly,
As redeemers become nemesis.
By the time you hit the floor,
Law enforcers had forgotten what they learnt at college.
The Chief ordered them to take days off.
Then transferred to far flung stations upon resumption.
A proof that the powerful elites reserve the right of one's erasure.
For, in this side of the world,
'Justice' keeps one eye open for the right price.
Walls beholden to no sound impenetrable barriers without resolve,
As your casket reached six feet down.
A restin' place that allowed you solitude denied on the surface.
But dear reader, lookin' at your brother's lifeless body…
A body riddled with sixteen bullet holes;
Is unlike lookin' at a vase filled with sixteen flowers,
While peein' in your grandmother's washroom!
So, I'll reveal what happened:
A promise to mother 'n self, I made.

The screams 'n echoes fade over-time.
But, gives way to questions when stillness becomes a mute horror;
When outcome hides truth from sight instillin' hopelessness.
With eyes deafened 'n ears blinded to sufferin',
Your death, dear brother, justified my principles.
It energized my resolve to shoulder on for:
Justice 'n fairness, integrity 'n inclusivity, love 'n hope for all…
But, on your thought dearest brother,
I still get a tear before I get a smile.
So, I'll reveal what happened: A promise I make.

32.9 I will Reveal what Happened: Promise I Make

Like a lost sheep, I approached the law enforcers.
To aid in revealin' the happenings of that horrendous night.
The night sixteen bullet's smoked my brother into spirit.
I gave them a benevolent smile…
In return, they gave atrocious stares – inconceivable 'n traumatic.
Their jest was both damp-squid 'n insipid.
In their presence, air became so stale that water sulked,
And, the sky was a viscous bloody mosaic.
The sulfurous fumes of sufferin' lingered.

> Armed with charged rubber cables,
> The drugged-up law-keepers mercilessly flogged;
> Dragged 'n made me dance to their abuses.
> They spread me wide on their devilish display chart.
> They promised to blow my brain,
> Then, insert their bloody-rusted knives into my hysterical arsehole.
> They momentarily shorn away my hope.
> Hope of revealin' the happenings of that night.
> I wept-fought away from their care.

> > Lost in the words,
> > I could scream not the truths that I had promised to reveal,
> > But, I could still see their reddish hands,
> > With my brother's fresh blood drippin' from their fingertips.
> > I decided to make red-ink out of it;
> > Transform it into peacefully profound truth -
> > So beautiful 'n breathlessly cadence to wish at the moment.

> The sure-fire way to kiss a touch of solace…
> And, reveal what happened…

Divin' deeper 'n deeper,
Climbin' steeper 'n steeper,
Desires ignited an inferno within.
The heat of its flames consumed the interior of my temple.
E'ery stare seemed like an attempt to unsee creation,
While words on a tongue sounded like rhythmic coughin'.
As time came to an inevitable halt.
Stay hopeful,
E'en though abused, truth must be revealed:
[I whispered to self.]
For the key to the truth remained locked in dark closets by the killers.
The truth that speaks the language of dark light 'n smoggy air.

> Outlivin' e'ery arrow;
> Outlastin' e'ery dagger;
> And, outwearin' e'ery bullet,
> That greeted me in their violent glory…
> After my lungs grew accustomed to their abuse,
> All I learned was how to hold my breath 'n cry underwater,
> As I painfully drowned in my resolve for (my brother's) justice.
> At last, they came for my neck at the wee-small-hours,
> But found that I had learnt how to fly…
> They questioned my portraits in loud but disrespectful tones.
> They worked their eager semi-automatic machine-guns silly,
> And, left gaping scars on my bedroom walls.

32.10 Learnt How to Fly

Before I learnt to fly 'n the words in me matured,
The dogs of war 'n hatred barked;
And, darkness enveloped me.
Lines were blurred while sound was muffled.
I saw life in a dull 'n dark way.
Laughter made me wish I was deaf.
Life took the shape of a torturous monster.
A monster that got louder when I tried not to listen.
What a body-mind-soul war!

Today, I hear birds rejoice.
The sky's serenity is upon the mountain seen:
The countryside smiles 'n bright runs the silver stream.
The Sun returns 'n with His magical smile illumes.
Life appears…
I hear flowers utter cries of joy;
And, breathe life into the sunup atop mountains.
I bathe naked in the streams,
Dance in the sundown;
And, enjoy explosive sex beneath twinklin' stars.
I travel far 'n wide,
Seekin' fresh experiences with those who dare run with the wind.
A thingy so pleasant 'n so dear!
I feel it…
The galaxy pamperin' my body,
Blanketin' the essence of my soul.
What an orgasmic feelin'!
That I feel…

Uprooted men hope for a livelihood that fits their expandin' sense of self.

Thus, I accept without complaint the toil.
The toil that is suited for the riot of my soul;
And, willingly devote my heart 'n soul to accomplishin'.
I seek, search 'n create what I can suppress not;
And, uplift self to a higher pitch 'n nurtures harmony within.
Radiatin' love for the rivers, mountains, sky 'n all earthlings.
For what matters in life is not a thingy,
But, the prevalence of the unreal o'er the real.

Smelt inner-peace on the breezes of the sky.
So, out of not cowardice –
I learnt to fly 'n flew to better my death.
And here, on exile fence, I dwell with nothin'.
Nothin' plausible to down me.
As the premature baby's still in the incubator;
And, a hurt heart heals,
But a healed heart hurts.
From this vantage point, I have learned regardless:
By workin' on self-improvement,
And dedicatin' life to purposeful goals,
One reaffirms the value of his existence.
This is the immediate fruit of uprootin':
Thus, I convert my tears of bitterness into a healin' serum;
By cultivatin' an artistic approach to life.
Alors!
Écrirai pour l'amour d'autrui.
Les flèches me perforent et fortifient,
Mon cœur elles font trembler de peur!

Notes for Poems 32.8, 32.9 and 32.10

Over the next several weeks, I was told in excruciatingly vivid details about the events that led up-to my brother's death. I learnt that my brother had a professional-related disagreement with his employer, a scion of a wealthy and political dynasty in Kenya. [My brother had detailed this disagreement to me a week before he was murdered.] In a pre-arranged manner, one of his colleagues invited him for an evening drink. At about midnight, he was tricked out of the building in downtown Nairobi - Kenya, and two undercover police officers forced him into a waiting car. The following morning, the police 'collected' his mutilated body at the edge of Karura Forest within Nairobi. According to the private post-mortem, my brother was heavily tortured. He was hit with a blunt object, read gun-butt, on the back of his head several times causing multiple fractures on the skull. Then, he was strangulated. As in many other similar cases in this part of the world, my brother was labelled a dangerous armed criminal.

After his burial, I promised my aging mother that I would do whatever it takes for justice to be done. I badly wanted to know what happened to my brother. Unearthing the specific details that lead to his killing was like peeling an onion. The outer skin came out with some difficulties, but in no time, I was in its innards, which caused tears to stream freely from my eyes, and my heart. It was like ripping open an old wound every second, every minute, every hour, and every day for months. The pain was, and remains, both palpable and excruciating.

Paradoxically, rather than offering answers, the information provided by the law enforcers raised more questions. Questions that remain unanswered for my family. The casual way the police officers treated our enquiries left us totally devastated.

After a while, the heat was turned on me. I was haunted and hunted. I was warned that if "I don't stop pursuing the killers, I'll be killed. I had to ran how to fly to save my life.

[Notes published with permission – Kibicho, 2019]

32.11 We Descend to Rise

Of all sadness this is sad…
But, it shall be as it e'er meant to be.
As nature disallows discontinuity.

Your brother's now part of nature's whole picture.
As he sits in his seat –
Next to the Master Sculptor.
So, take a long-slow-high thespian breath.

Be grateful for whatever comes.
For, all's ordered as a guide from beyond.
And, your loved one lives on…
He can die not 'til the ripples he caused die.

32.12 Death of a Child

My heart aches for you,
For, there's no greater sorrow –
To find a child gone.

>Trust in His wisdom divine.
>And, bask in the comfort,
>Of the treasured moments you shared.

>>Trust in His wisdom divine.
>>Smile a little and often…
>>And, you'll begin to heal.

32.13 Lives in Another's Heart

Life of the dead is placed on the memories of the living.
Love given in life keeps givers alive beyond their time.
For, anyone who gives love,
Lives on in another's heart.

~ Marcus Cicero (106 - 43 BC) ~

PART THREE

CONCLUSIONS

The
Melody
Has to end
To reach its goal.

Chapter 33

End

Every ending's a new beginning.

~ Lao Tzu (571 – 447 BC) ~

33.1 The Melody has to End to Reach its Goal

Endings usher beginnings.
For life ends not.
The trick being:

To recognize when a life-stage's o'er;
And, to leave without denying its validity.
To have a sense of future;
And, to believe that e'ery exit's an entry.

For, the end of a melody isn't its goal,
But, the melody has to end to reach its goal.
…A melody of fairness;
For, fairness' in action,
Not in wordin'.

33.2 Fairness is in Action

Endings to be useful must be inconclusive.
So, I rest our journey by instructin':
Live fairness, profess it not.
For, fairness' in action,
Not in wordin'.

I rest our journey by notin':
Seek 'n leave jollity in e'ery path you tread;
For, fairness' in action,
Not in wordin'.

I rest our journey by repeatin':
Make others feel that there's somethin' in them.
For, fairness' in action,
Not in wordin'.

33.3 Have no Time to Hate

O' dear reader,
As our journey come to an end;
Be as enthusiastic about the success of the 'other'.
As you're about yours.

> As *Live Well: Reveal Your Soul* comes to a closure;
> Be the good you expect in 'other';
> Be the light you expect to see in the 'other.
> Give so much time to self-improvement,
> That you've no time to hate.
>
>> Have no time to hate.
>> Be a greater human being.
>> And, the world shall be –
>> More equal 'n fair to all.

REFERENCES

Aristotle (384 - 322 BC). *Nicomachean Ethics.* Books VIII and IX (1155-1172a)

Gouldner, A. (1960) 'The Norm of Reciprocity'. *American Sociological Review.* 25: 161-78.

Hardy, T. (1994) *The Convergence of the Twain: The lacking Sense (Collected Poems).* Wordsworth Editions, United Kingdom.

Kibicho, W. (2019) *Beyond Negative Ethnicity, Corruption and Violence: In Salvage of Africa's Soul.* Sakata Publications, Canada.

Plato (424 - 348 BC) *Republic.* Books I and II.

ABOUT THE AUTHOR

Dr. Wanjohi Kibicho, Ph.D. has over twenty years of university teaching experience. He has published widely on tourism management, sex tourism, sustainable tourism and traditional martial arts. Dr. Kibicho also does international consultancy in all aspects of the tourism industry. He is a perfervid traditional martial artist who stresses the benefits of the art towards body-mind-soul enlightenment. As a poet, he is devoted to empowering human beings to love and appreciate the interconnectedness of nature.

Dr. Kibicho has travelled extensively and from time to time has sojourned in Leeuwarden (the Netherlands), Karlstad (Sweden), Lyon (France), Pretoria (South Africa) and Ottawa (Canada). He has been close to the roots of philosophical consciousness through his travels and his work as a researcher and writer. He poses the humane eye for the less privileged and degradation of humanity.

www.ingramcontent.com/pod-product-compliance
Lightning Source LLC
Chambersburg PA
CBHW050554170426
43201CB00011B/1689